Slants of Light

Stories and Poems From
The Women's Writing Circle

Margaret —
I love your wonderful
sense of humor — your joyful
energy —
What a pleasure it is to
know you —
        Harriet

There's a certain Slant of light,
Winter Afternoons —
That oppresses, like the Heft
Of Cathedral Tunes —

                    Emily Dickinson

Contents

Motherhood | 49

Foreword

As long as I have been a writer, I wanted to tell women's stories.

As a journalist, I interviewed women who managed school districts, administered nonprofits, directed efforts to save the landscape, organized healthcare consortiums for the working poor. In many ways, these women were my mentors. Their voices inspired me. Their courage and convictions initiated needed action to bring about change.

But it wasn't until after I started the Women's Writing Circle in November 2009 that I began asking myself *why this lifelong interest in stories about women?* The simplest answer I found was not unique for a writer: I had a story I wanted – and needed – to tell.

After I left my career in journalism, I found little stopping me from following another rhythm to my days. I could write about my own life.

And so I began writing my memoirs. Along the way, I gradually found "my voice" – as a woman – with apologies to no one – just the truth as best I could tell it.

Our Circle expanded from a small handful to a dozen or more women at our monthly readings, and I realized I wasn't alone. Other women confided, first in whispers and then in assertive voices to each other, and to me, that they, too, longed to break the silence and tell their stories.

As they began writing their most defining moments, reading and discussing them aloud and getting immediate reaction, they said it felt as if a long-sealed window had been thrown open and light burst into the room.

This anthology has been fed by the revelations and discoveries shared in the readings. It grew out of a rather innocent question on my part one sunny April morning in 2012 at the Women's Writing Circle. As we sipped our coffee and tea from bright red ceramic mugs, a small candle in the center of a book-laden table burned brightly, releasing warm scents of vanilla and spice. I had been listening to stories of pain and fear, triumph and tragedy, each woman sharing her memories in a variety of approaches: either through fiction, creative non-fiction, memoir, or poetry. When each woman read her story, her power and honesty impressed me.

I heard myself ask, "What do you think about sharing some of our stories in a published anthology?"

A few heads turned to one another. One woman asked, "Would anyone care what we have to say?"

"We'll never know if we don't try," answered another.

And so, after patient, soul-searching determination, clarifying of thoughts, writing, rewriting, editing, and pure nerve . . . *Slants of Light: Stories and Poems From the Women's Writing Circle* reaches out to you, the reader.

Our stories and poems reflect the scope and diversity of the contributors in the Women's Writing Circle, whose ages range from late 20s to a senior of 70 years. We come from many different careers and backgrounds. Some of our words evoke the stories of countless women growing up in the challenging feminist generation when the phrase, "You can have it all," drove many pursuits, dreams and careers.

School teachers, journalists, office workers, mothers - many succeeded beyond their wildest dreams. Some put dreams aside. Some found duty demanding and stifling. In their individual pursuits, some remained true to tradition. Others rebelled, placing their energies into newer, different visions of spirit and power; into the power of themselves.

Here and there in this collection, you will share friendships, different points of view, a longing for connection. A woman senses her partner's harsh speaking tone, and steadies her resolve. Another dips a toe into the world of online dating. The whispers from a beloved grandfather... the slam of a screen door as a mother calls her child in for dinner...the wonder of a butterfly alighting on a little girl's arm – this is our anthology. Each "slant of light" creates its own mystery and magic, dream and fantasy, delight and marvel. Each "passing snowflake" suggests a symbol of the frailty, tenacity and fortitude of women's voices.

I often think of the unspoken words of women throughout the ages – women who never got the chance to tell their stories – women who, like my mother's generation, were not so much suppressed as censored by society's unspoken code – that women should remain voiceless.

Virginia Woolf wrote in *A Room of One's Own* of the collective consciousness of all women as they travel the journey of the feminine: "She lived in you and in me, and in many other women who are not here tonight, for they are washing up the dishes and putting the children to bed."

And so, my hope is that our voices echo the voices of the women who came before us and will come after us. I believe our stories and poems illustrate a courageous attempt to support and advance the woman's voice within and that – individually and collectively – we will contribute to our understanding of one another and the world around us. Together, we belong to one grand group working out through our particular writing the vital and universal themes of a woman's many-faceted life.

Susan G. Weidener
January 27, 2013

Last Shot at the Brass Ring

By Susan G. Weidener

As soon as Emma parked the car and got out, he started walking toward her. Disheveled hair, Donald Trump comb-over style, wrinkled blue denim shirt and tan khakis that looked as though he had slept in them. Gorgeous blue eyes.

An Internet date. One of many she had been on over the years. As she rode the merry-go-round of dating, she hoped timing and luck might conspire to bring her within reach of the elusive brass ring. She remembered riding the carousel on the boardwalk in Ocean City, New Jersey when she was a little girl. A metal arm swung out holding a brass ring. There was only one ring for each ride and everyone tried to grab it so they could redeem it for the grand prize, a free ride. Now the prize she sought was love, connection, emotional support. She sometimes scoffed at her own wishful thinking; some might even call it a fantasy at this stage of life.

After a brief phone conversation – in which he had told her he was a writer, they had agreed to meet.

"Emma!" he said, stepping forward to hug her.

She hated the touching. Just because she had agreed to brunch, it was still courteous to wait to get to know someone first. Or maybe they touched because they hoped for arousal. Sam was 60 years old. Unless men were on Viagra or Cialis, sexual arousal often proved elusive as any number of infirmities from high blood pressure, diabetes, knee surgery, even bouts with cancer took their toll.

They walked into the restaurant and were seated at a table with purple chrysanthemums in a glass bowl. After they returned from the brunch buffet, he started to pull the clams out of the half shell, then lick his fingers of their bay seasoning. She watched as he rubbed his fingers on the white linen napkin, leaving a pale orange stain. Then he rolled the napkin into a ball and put it next to his plate.

"So . . . tell me. How long has your husband been dead?"

She dreaded the question, but knew it was part of the introduction since *widowed* was on her Internet profile. There was no way around it. Sam pursued, wanting to know if she had any relationships since David's death.

Was this man a moron?

"Of course. I just didn't love them," she said.

———— ◦ ————

She often wondered what she and David would be doing with their lives, saying to each other this morning if things had turned out differently. Aging together . . . slowly and gracefully, or so she imagined.

Sam told her she looked as pretty in person as her picture on the Internet dating site. The picture Emma had posted had been taken on a sunny day on her deck. Her hair had a kind of ethereal glow; her face looked almost youthful, helped along by enough Estee Lauder facial creams and ointments that her purchases over the years should have earned her major stockholder status in the company.

Emma remembered what Bette Davis had once said, "I may be in the body of an 80 year-old, but I am looking out of the eyes of a 16-year-old girl."

Emma wasn't eighty, but she was precariously teetering away from even the middle-aged bracket. She hoped to stay youthful-looking for as long as she could, but then what? The Botox route? Never say never. Society had no use for aging, particularly when it came to women. When a woman turned forty, it started, growing worse with each succeeding year until at fifty a woman was virtually invisible . . . unless you were Madonna or Michelle Pfeiffer. Men no longer looked at you when you walked into a room; certainly there were no more wolf whistles, which was a good thing. Employers shuffled past your resume. At fifty-six, Emma sometimes felt as old as Methuselah, weighed down by too much cynicism and emotional fatigue, the inevitable result of being a woman in a man's world and a reporter most of her life until recently.

As Sam continued to lick his fingers, Emma felt slightly nauseous. She wanted to quietly escape, never to do this again. Dating had become like chewing gum: The longer and harder you did it, the more tasteless it became, especially the older you got. Then it began to veer toward the pathetic. Shouldn't you have figured out by a certain age the advantages of staying single? Although Emma did like her independence and owning her own home, it could get lonely when there was no one to go to the theater with or drive to the country. Which is why she was still on the Internet. Hopeful, always hopeful, never willing to give in to being alone for the rest of her life. Although what did you call the man you dated when you were fifty-something and he was sixty or older? A man friend? A partner? Certainly not a boyfriend!

Sam told Emma that he was twice divorced; well, not exactly, since he and the second wife had not yet signed off on the papers.

Emma's alarm must have registered on her face.

"Oh, we haven't been together for a long time. That's over," he said, quickly adding he lived alone, although his grown children often visited.

Emma was annoyed. She made it a rule never to date them if they had checked *currently separated* on their Internet profile. Too much baggage.

But what came next was more alarming; a long-winded explanation of how he was intent on finding a cure for war and developing world peace. He had this notion, he said, that the UN Security Council needed complete revamping and he knew how to do it.

Sam claimed he had gotten an audience years before with a former high-ranking Clinton official to broach his proposal — make Britain the chief arbiter of the Council, and go out on a world tour speaking engagement promoting the idea. Apparently, the Clinton advisor gave him encouragement, but after a short trip to India, Sam returned to Pennsylvania.

———— ◦◉◦ ————

Emma didn't have the energy to question him about any of it. And her recently self-published memoir on love and loss hardly compared to a book he was penning on world peace and the need for mankind to live collectively, holistically, and in brotherhood. Had she just stepped back to 1969 and Woodstock?

Should she head back for the roast turkey breast or the steamed shrimp?

———— ◦◉◦ ————

"You know," Sam was saying, "I like you. You are very nice, intelligent and understated."

Emma jerked back to attention. "What do you mean by understated?"

"Not flamboyant," he said with a grin.

He went on to explain that he had been dating a woman from Minnesota he met on the Internet. She was into crystals and Buddhism. She also enjoyed phone sex. Sam, however, was tiring of the lack of intimacy that phone sex offered, or rather, didn't.

He was also "seeing" a psychiatrist, not for therapy, though. He had met her on the Internet and they had become "friends." He didn't feel that way about her, although she did about him.

"She's willing to accept that?" Emma asked, thinking this merely reaffirmed her opinion that psychiatrists rarely had their act together.

"We like each other," he said. "And we agree that this is what's wrong with marriage, the whole institution of marriage. It's like an 'us against them' mentality. I believe in loving everyone and not inhibiting someone with a piece of paper. Why not give them the freedom to be who they are?"

———◉———

"Emma! How are you?"

A group of people from Emma's church had just entered the dining room. Emma wanted to crawl under the table. Here she was with Doc the Mad Scientist from *Back to the Future*, hair sticking up, finger-licking-holistic-peace-guru, twice married yet thinking marriage inhibited one's karma. All she needed now was to hear him tell these people from church that he had invented a plutonium-powered time machine.

One woman, openly eyeing Sam, asked Emma if she could give her name to a friend who was thinking of writing a memoir. Emma regularly attended church alone, and seeing her with a man must have come as a surprise.

"Of course," Emma hastily responded, realizing she had forgotten the woman's name. She had always been terrible with names, and the older she got, the worse it was. Not remembering her name made it easier to skip introducing Sam.

With huge relief, Emma watched them wander off to be seated in another part of the restaurant.

"You know there is something I haven't told you," Sam said.

Oh no. What else? Wasn't phone sex, the fact that he wasn't divorced, his belief he could come up with a formula for world peace enough?

"I believe I may be the Prophet Elijah."

Come again, she thought to herself? *Who the heck was the Prophet Elijah anyway?*

"You do know who that is, don't you?" Sam asked, seeing her dumbfounded expression.

"Ah . . ."

"He predicted the world would come to an end in a cataclysm of fire. He would return before that happened." Sam said if she wanted, he would show her passages from the Bible that linked him as Elijah.

Emma's one thought was the line out of *Annie Hall* where Alvy, played by Woody Allen, says to Annie's crazy brother, "Excuse me, but I'm due back on the Planet Earth."

"Don't you believe the world is on the verge of catastrophe?" Sam asked.

Should she dash out now? Or tell him she believed she was Mary Magdalene?

Instead, Emma excused herself and on the way to the ladies room grabbed the waitress.

"Check, please," she said, pointing to Sam who was licking his fingers.

———◦———

Sam asked if she'd like to take in a movie with him sometime. Did the Prophet Elijah engage in such mundane activities when the world was coming to an end? Demurring that she would soon be taking a trip to China — actually, the trip was two months away! — Emma said maybe.

She had always hated hurting anyone's feelings even though when the check came, he noted that men and women should be equals in all respects, and if she wanted to offer her credit card, he wouldn't object. She hid a grimace and bit her tongue. She plunked down a $10 tip. She figured if she'd had to listen to his tales of phone sex and the Prophet Elijah, the least he could do was pick up the $40 tab.

"Here give me a hug," he said, as they walked out of the restaurant and she fumbled in her purse for the keypad to unlock her car. Before Emma could protest, Sam embraced her in a bear hug, no doubt to get a feel of her boobs pressing against his chest.

As she drove home past the familiar open fields, subdivisions, and strip malls, Emma tried to remain philosophical. Somewhere in all those endless listings of photographs and descriptions of hopefuls, there might be one good guy who knew how to comb his hair and press his shirt. A guy who wasn't narcissistic enough to believe himself an Old Testament prophet or the answer to world peace.

Love is just one big crapshoot anyway, she thought, watching the trees and houses slide by the car window. *All it takes is one person to turn it all around and offer you his hand — preferably licked of bay seasoning.*

She might be convinced to reach out her hand, too — one last shot at the brass ring.

The Legacy of a Childless Woman

By Patty Kline-Capaldo

It was Grandma Capaldo's 103rd birthday party. As the family began to fill up the tiny Italian restaurant for the annual event, I studied a beautiful painting of the family tree, a gift from one of her grandchildren. The trunk stood thick and strong, shooting up into seven main branches. Each bough held the names of her children; then their children and grandchildren branched out from there. My father-in-law's branch yielded two offshoots. One continued into two more. Then there was ours, Rich's and mine. It just stopped. Chopped off. Ended. Finito. I turned away and sat in the back of the room. Seeing that visual depiction of the end of us, my husband and me, was like witnessing my own death.

What will I leave to the world?

With the party swirling around me, I poured myself wine and let my mind drift back over the past fifteen years. Sitting in the loft amidst the stroller, the high chair, and the other baby paraphernalia, I sobbed until I couldn't breathe. It was time to let go. It would never happen — not to me, not to us.

We had gotten a late start, so there was no secret that we'd try to get pregnant right away. You get married; you have children. That's the way it goes, isn't it? Sometimes it's backwards, but the point is, when you get married, especially in your late thirties, people expect you to get pregnant pretty quickly. So did I.

When a friend at work offered me those baby items, I readily accepted.

"I know you'll be needing these things soon. I'm done with them," she laughed. "No more for me, so you're welcome to them."

I hugged her and thanked her for her generosity, never doubting her predictions.

My family also had high expectations. Every time I spoke to my mother, my sister, my brother or his wife, I could sense they were anticipating an announcement. I felt like I was letting them down.

Rich and I had started trying to get pregnant on our wedding night. A few months later, I began charting my ovulation cycle, so we could time our lovemaking to the best advantage. I would even elevate my hips afterwards to give the little swimmers some help. After about a year, we got tested.

Like so many women, it's my nature to protect. *I'll hide my pain so I don't make yours worse.* People assumed something was wrong with me. I resented that, but I didn't reveal the secret.

I felt like less of a woman, but I didn't want Rich to feel like less of a man. He rarely heard me as I cried silently beside him while he slept. It's not really his fault; he didn't know the depths of my devastation. I bottled it all up inside. I shut it down.

I wanted a baby. My husband didn't. At least he didn't want one badly enough to take extreme measures. If it had happened naturally, he would have welcomed a child and been a wonderful father. But at forty years old, he wasn't willing to begin the long, arduous, and expensive undertaking of in vitro fertilization or adoption.

We were married a long time before I faced my lingering resentments about that. He had no idea, because I didn't let him see. I had fallen back on an old coping mechanism my family called *clamming up*.

When I gave away those baby things to Rich's pregnant sister, she asked, "Are you sure you're okay with this?"

How different things might have been if I'd been honest and said, "Of course not. I'll never be okay."

But I shut it down. She never knew that I huddled on her bathroom floor and cried the day her little girl got baptized.

Many days I wanted to scream. I'd waited so long to get married, waiting for the right one. *Was this some kind of cosmic joke? Not funny, God!*

I actually thought about balling up my hand into a fist and slamming it into the wall with all my might. Anticipation of the pain stopped me. But maybe the physical pain would have been preferable to the strangling, suffocating ache in my heart. I had mothered so many other people's children, friends and family. My brother and sister each had two boys and, from day one, I loved them as my own. I treasured being Aunt Patty, but I wanted to be Mom. But that dream was not to be. How do you survive the death of a dream? The same way you survive any death: denial, anger, isolation, depression, and eventually, acceptance.

I was so pissed at God. He'd promised me. I knew it. I had felt it in my bones, in my essence. My turn would come. Those reassurances — that "still small voice" — turned out to be a lie. That was the deadliest thing: Losing that trust in my intuition, the inner knowing that had guided me through my life choices. I tried to hold on to my belief, sitting in church trying to worship, aching and angry. It was so unfair. All the people who abused or even killed their kids, and God couldn't trust me?

Why didn't I scream or hit the wall? Because I was a good little girl, and good little girls don't throw tantrums. I kept it all inside. And I got fat. I ate my way through the depression. I gained three pant sizes and four bra sizes.

I had always been proud of my figure. It was tied to my sexuality, my womanhood, my sense of self. Even so, there were times in my life when I was so self-conscious, I would hesitate to walk across a room in front of men. I had drawn unwanted attention so often. I would almost shrink inside myself to hide.

Now, hidden behind layers of excess flesh, I was comfortable for the first time in years. I could talk to men and joke and even flirt, and they wouldn't get the wrong idea. But now I wonder if there's another connection. The blow to my womanhood of not having a baby — of never even getting pregnant — may have led me to gain weight and hide my womanhood behind fat and frumpy clothes.

I remember one dress in particular. It was purple with tiny flowers on it and had a pleated skirt that only emphasized my girth. Long sleeves and a high neckline completed the matronly look. When I caught my reflection in my office window, I didn't recognize the woman I'd become.

I had landed a new job. The new surroundings, new people, and new responsibilities enabled me to distance myself from my maternal longings. I threw myself into my work, and it saved me. Being busy saved me. In my cubicle where I compiled reports, surrounded by boxes, darkness in the window, finishing up a twelve-hour day, I didn't have time to think about being sad.

Years passed, and the depression slowly receded like darkness before the dawn. Action. I highly recommend it. Grieve, mourn, rage — feel the pain. Then get up and move.

The extra weight had started to affect my health. I had trouble getting out of my car. My hips hurt, my knees hurt, my feet hurt. Emerging from the emotional pain, I wanted to be free of the physical pain too.

I lost the weight — three dress sizes, but only one bra size. Those oversized symbols of motherhood seemed to mock me; they also hurt my back. So I opted for breast reduction surgery to cut away the remnants of my façade and get me back to my natural size. I felt good about myself again. Confident. Sexy. But I had needed that place to hide in plain sight while I morphed into someone new.

Even while I was learning to accept the reality of being childless, I would still get a buildup of hope every month, only to be disappointed when my period came. And just when I thought I was safe from that biological clock — no more periods, no more monthly reminder — now I could move on and enjoy those mature years, then — Bam! The conversations turned from children to grandchildren and, once again, I found myself longing to hold a baby in my arms. That's when I realized it would never end. I would always be an outsider, different from society's norm.

Motherhood is natural; it's normal, which makes me unnatural, abnormal — a freak. That reality struck me once again as I watched the festivities at Grandma's birthday party. I stood on the edge of the circle watching grandmothers and mothers dance with their children. The feeling of being on the outside looking in overwhelmed me once again.

When it was time for the traditional family portrait, we all crowded around Grandma. This tiny woman, strong as an oak, silver hair perfectly coiffed, nails painted a daring red, was surrounded by scores of her offspring.

When I think of women who never had children, I think of Oprah and Mother Theresa and the amazing impact they've had on the world. We can't all live our lives on such a grand scale, but we can touch the lives of those around us.

How do you survive the death of a dream? You find another dream. I searched for an outlet, some way to let my voice be heard and to leave my mark on the world in my own small way. In my search, I rediscovered a passion I had buried for many years. I started to write, and something quickened inside of me. A revival of that innate knowledge that told me I was on the right path.

My stories are my babies now. I'm pregnant with them. I know the moment they were conceived. I feel them kicking, turning around inside me (no, it's not just gas). I hear their heartbeats. Their conception was anything but immaculate. They were conceived out of the pain and loss and love and joy that is my life. I will labor to see them born with my blood, sweat, and tears. And then I will mother them, nurture them, raise them up, and send them out to make their way in the world.

Career

Live Your Dream!

By Ginger Murphy

Serena and Carla sat sipping chilled Chardonnay in Carla's summer garden. As they often did when something big happened in their lives, Carla and Serena sat and talked. This time, Carla had lost her job. Serena pulled the folded newspaper section gently out from under a basket on the table where they were sitting.

"You're supposed to be reading job postings, not obituaries! What's the matter with you, anyway?" Serena prodded, filling her glass from the nearby wine bottle. "Sometimes I think you come from another universe."

"Haven't you ever wondered what people will write about you when you're gone?" Carla asked.

"No, not really," Serena answered, a quizzical look on her face. "Then again," she mused, "you're Irish so that automatically means you've got a morbid streak."

Carla smiled. Her friend knew her well. Tragedy was part of her roots, so maybe a fascination with the macabre was in her blood. More than anything, she identified with the suffering of dispossessed, left-out, and discarded people. Maybe that was why she related with such empathy to the kids in special education who had been the focus of her recent work. Although she had only been out of work for two months, she felt the pain of being outside the mainstream, used up and thrown away when no longer useful, or — in these tough economic times - affordable.

Five years ago, Carla had been promoted to educational services director at Catch a Star Foundation's office in Philadelphia. It was a new position, and she was charged with the development of innovative school-based reading programs and with training the program's volunteer staff. Carla was thrilled to be breaking new ground.

All told, Carla spent ten years with Catch a Star, and her colleagues had become a second family. They celebrated birthdays, holidays, marriages and babies together. They mourned the loss of loved ones, failed marriages, and colleagues who had been laid off. When funding streams dried up in the Great Recession, the national foundation seemed to change overnight. Ten years ago, it was a nonprofit focused on serving kids. Now, it seemed more like a corporation concerned only with its own survival.

As funding ran out, there was no money to continue paying her salary. Instead, her teachers and volunteers would be trained and supervised by an online instructor from the Foundation's headquarters office in New York. *So much for the personalized and customized training they'd promised the teachers who had signed up for the program,* Carla thought to herself. A one-size-fits-all plan taught by a stranger in another city was now all the Foundation could offer. It was a far cry from the days when she visited each campus and met regularly with teachers, many of whom she had known for years.

She let out a long sigh. At this point, she felt tired and overwhelmed. Three years ago she had buried her husband of 17 years after his five-year battle with cancer. Along with Serena, her co-workers had been her lifeline after John died. Now as she lost this beloved group of colleagues in the aftermath of lay-offs, she realized this was yet another death.

———— ◉ ————

"What if we actually wrote our own obituary ahead of time?" Carla mused. "That way, we'd already know what we want to accomplish. Then we'd be ready to write a resume based on the job we wanted to find instead of trying to fit ourselves into the first job that came along."

"I don't know, Rini," Carla continued, using her friend's childhood nickname. "I just want things to be real. I am so tired of all the bullshit and trying to work around people's egos just to get things accomplished."

"Oh honey, I hear you. You always were one to cut to the quick of the matter," Rini reflected.

———— ◉ ————

So much had changed since the two women embarked on careers to change the world. In college, they had endless late-night discussions over coffee and imagined their lives in five, ten, and twenty years. They felt such conviction and certainty then. The fact that they could and would make their mark was not in question. Now things were not so clear and felt anything but certain. The economic fallout from the Great Recession seemed endless; they knew neighbors, friends, and family who had lost jobs, health insurance and pension plans in its wake.

Then there were life events like death, divorce, and illness that were definitely not part of the original plan. With each blow, somehow it felt harder and harder to begin again. At some point, their career focus shifted from what fed their hearts to what filled their wallets. Both women had made compromises for what they believed were jobs that would provide financial security and at least some measure of professional satisfaction.

Before deciding to accept the Catch a Star job, Carla debated long and hard. Should she leave the part-time job she loved at the local after-school program she had created for the security of a full-time position with an enviable benefits package?

Serena, whose passion was summer camp programming for girls, soon realized that sustaining herself and her son on three part-time jobs without benefits just so she could go back to camp the next summer was not a sane option. Eventually, she settled for a coaching career at Girls' High in Philadelphia. At least there she could be outside most of the time while helping girls build their confidence and leadership skills in the competitive sports arena.

———◆———

Serena sighed. "So," she ventured, "any ideas about what's next?"

"Honestly," Carla replied, "I don't. I used to have so many ideas. I used to think people would be interested in my ideas and what I had to say. Now, I feel most of the time people nod and smile as if they're listening but they're not. Maybe if I go out to the nearest street corner and start stripping I might get some attention."

"Ah, yes, "Serena responded. "I guess they'll always be a market for our skills in that arena, right?"

"Listen to us!" Carla exclaimed, sitting bolt upright in her chair. "We sound like we're done! Take us out of the oven, please!"

Darkness gently seeped into the sky and lightning bugs appeared, dotting the landscape like pulsing glitter. Serena took a matchbook out of her purse and reached for the citronella candle in a small silver bucket on the chair next to her. With a forceful scrape, she lit a match and placed it over the wick of the candle. As Carla rose from her chair to get another bottle of wine, the phone that she had perched in the kitchen window at the end of the garden walk began to ring.

"Ugh! Should I get that?" she asked, looking at Serena, who pointed both thumbs down, mimicking a pained expression.

Sighing, Carla hurried up the walkway and disappeared inside.

Serena was left to ruminate while staring into the flame of the lone candle, which now sat in the middle of the table glowing softly. It's so unfair, she thought. Carla has worked so hard all these years. But working hard is not enough. Having a stellar performance record is not enough. Taking on more responsibilities with less pay is not enough. God, she thought, how pathetic that it all gets reduced to numbers, and when your number is up, you go.

"Guess what?" Carla called through the kitchen window.

Serena turned to see her friend waving a piece of paper on the other side of the screen. "What?" she answered cautiously.

Carla pushed the door open with her shoulder, a basket of pretzels balanced in one arm and a fresh bottle of white wine in the other.

"So that was Stan at Catch a Star and he said they posted a new position at the New York office on Friday."

"You have to be kidding me. You would not actually consider working again for the same place that just dumped you, right?"

"I don't know. The funny thing is, it's same the position I begged them to create because I knew it could support the school programs we wanted to start with our teachers in Philly. Hell, I practically wrote the job description they've posted! I just printed it out from Stan's e-mail," she said, waving a sheet of paper triumphantly.

"You would seriously consider this position? After everything that's happened?" Serena's voice started to rise in pitch.

"And you do realize that you'd be working with the angels of death again?" she added, for dramatic flair.

They had given the human resources director and her assistants this moniker after the second round of layoffs when they appeared unannounced in offices across the country to begin the cutbacks. After proffering a manila envelope with the requisite legal documents to each newly "released" employee, the "angels" accompanied these poor souls to their desks with strict instructions to turn in keys and business cards, pack up personal belongings and leave immediately. Carla would never forget the starkness of losing her professional identity with this set of rote gestures; you walked in the building as a professional and out the door as an unemployment statistic.

After they settled in at the table again, Carla sat staring at the email. "Okay," Carla said slowly.

Serena felt uneasy as she watched her friend. She held her breath, waiting for either an argument in favor of returning to the organization or fallout from the crushing realization that this was an absurd idea after all. She was totally unprepared for what came next.

"What if," Carla continued, "what if I just forget the Foundation and keep the job posting?"

"And do what with it?!" Serena asked, looking increasingly skeptical.

"Well, it's the job I've always wanted, Rini. You know working with volunteers is where my heart is."

Carla got up from her chair and walked into the garden where she gently captured one of the lightning bugs in her hands. She returned to the table and sat down, spreading her fingers just enough to see the glow inside without releasing the tiny creature.

"Just exactly when did we stop dreaming, Rini?" she queried. "What was the point at which we actually gave up on what we loved?"

"Maybe this whole economic meltdown is just some big reassignment going on, " Carla suggested, "and now I am finally getting a chance to find the organization that will hire me for the job I've created. Maybe I am the one who is supposed to be interviewing company candidates that I'll hire to help me with my own mission. How's that for a cosmic re-frame?" she asked, looking over at Serena whose expression reflected a mixture of bemusement and affection.

Serena gazed at the tiny pulsations of light inside Carla's hands. Her friend exasperated and fascinated her at the same time. She could not quite get her mind around it, but Carla had this quality of endurance that helped her weather the storms while still being able to imagine, in the midst of the gale, a time when the skies would clear and the seas would again be tranquil. And it wasn't in some clueless Pollyanna way where you knew she was oblivious. She knew the score. It's just that she didn't focus on it as the ultimate result.

"I've got to hand it to you, girl, you don't let the jerks get you down," Serena responded.

"Look," Carla continued, "Maybe they've done me a big favor by cutting me loose. You know how tied up in knots I've been over trying to make management understand what teachers in the field have been telling us they needed in programs and staff. Catch a Star's board led me to think they were truly interested in the blueprints my volunteer advisory committee created, and that the grant we secured was in fact earmarked for program implementation. Then the ax fell, and I realized they never even intended to fund the program in the first place."

"You wouldn't have left unless they had let you go, right?" Serena said, more as a statement of fact than an actual question.

"You know I'm a die-hard, Rini."

"Yeah, I do know that about you," she laughed.

Carla lifted her cupped hands, opening them slowly to release the lightening bug. Her eyes swelled with tears.

Serena put down her glass, leaned over and reached toward her. Carla extended her arms, enfolding Serena's slim shoulders. They sat in silence.

"We just can't give up, Rini," Carla pleaded more to herself than her friend. "We can't give up on the kids. We can't give up on our dream of teaching so every kid can learn. We've got to remind the adults in this world that if kids aren't learning, that's on us. Remember how we vowed that every kid matters?"

"I remember," Serena answered softly.

Carla felt as if her upwelling of grief was starting to mingle gradually with budding hope in a disorienting but somehow oddly clarifying way. She now realized that if she had stayed at Catch a Star her dream might have died altogether. She might have compromised for the sake of keeping the job instead of capturing her dream. She finally realized she would not have been able to implement her program there at all; after all, that door slammed shut as soon as the organization went into crisis mode.

Now that she was unemployed with no job to lose, she could open her imagination to new possibilities again. As she watched the lightning bugs glowing all around them, she hugged Serena more tightly. Carla realized that in this new beginning, her dreams were still very much alive.

Heavenly Baseball Diamond

By Jan L. Backes

I was depressed over a pass I'd made. The woman's name was Marcia. She was stunned when I tried to kiss her.

"Jan," she said. "I'm not gay. I like you but I just don't feel that way about you."

Marcia was someone I had been sharing an apartment with in a TLA—transitional living arrangement. We had lived together as part of a program sponsored by Penndel Psychiatric Center where both of us were being treated for severe depression.

Several women lived in the apartment for six months with minimal assistance. The ultimate goal was to have us branch out on our own. In the end, the project proved a failure because we were not self-sufficient enough psychologically or financially to make it in the world.

Dejected and embarrassed by Marcia's rejection, and after learning that a friend had betrayed my confidence by telling my mother I was gay, I got into my car and sped off. I didn't care where I ended up. After driving around for what felt like hours, I found myself sitting in Washington Crossing State Park, on the 'Jersey' side, not far from where I grew up in Levittown, Pennsylvania. I remembered my dad taking me to the Pennsy side of the park when I was a kid. We were inseparable, he and I. I went everywhere he went and, when I was very small, I stood next to him on the seat of his truck with my arm around his neck. Finding out I was gay was upsetting and confusing to him, and he could not accept my homosexuality.

I was sweating. My brown bangs stuck to my forehead. As I sat, I sobbed until I could hardly breathe. Mucus streamed from my nose, and I wiped it on my sleeve. After getting myself together, I drove off. This time I knew where I was headed. In the bedroom of my third roommate, Jen, was a bottle of her psyche meds. We were allowed to have our meds in the apartment. They weren't locked up. I had seen it on her dresser earlier that day. Jen had decided she wasn't going to take her psyche meds—ever, and they were just sitting there—so I grabbed them.

I picked the bottle up and shook it. It was full. I read the label, qty. 50. I guzzled the pills in one gulp with a 16-ounce can of Pabst Blue Ribbon beer. I don't know who brought it into the apartment, but it was there and I chugged it.

Almost immediately, my insides wretched. I began to tremble. My palms turned sweaty and my mouth dry. Thoughts ran through my mind... *God, I feel like you've turned your back on me. I would pray that you are not the mean, punishing God I knew from childhood.* Tears streamed down my cheeks as I sat in the empty bedroom. If the Catholic Church, which taught me about God, and my own father would not accept me, I felt I had nowhere to turn. Let down by the priests and nuns, the psychiatric community, and my parents, I felt lost.

In that pivotal moment I had to decide between living and dying. I realized I might have made the biggest mistake of all by trying to kill myself. I had to believe that I wasn't worthless because if I didn't, I would die. I called the psychiatric center. I hoped my therapist might answer the phone and save me. Nikki was out of the office. I identified myself.

"I've taken a bottle of my roommate's meds," I slurred into the phone.

"Well, Janis," the male voice on the other end replied, "You must hang up so that I can call an ambulance for you."

I did what I was told, but I wished I could have told this stranger on the other end of the phone how desperate I felt, how determined I was to kill the thing I thought would send me to hell.

The year was 1977, and few people knew about my struggle or the struggle of people like me. While the economy prospered and the country had experienced the free love and peace movement, even the Women's Movement, society had silenced those of us who were gay.

My sexual orientation didn't have a name for me back then; I'd never heard the word *lesbian*. But I knew the pain of not being accepted, and that was enough to make me want to die. I thought about my death a lot.

As I was rushed by ambulance to St. Mary's Hospital in nearby Newtown, I drifted in and out of consciousness and remembered back to those times, periods in my short life, when I'd known this same, terrifying measure of loneliness.

Once at the hospital I heard a nurse comment, "Damn! She's only a kid!"

At age twenty, I looked like a teenage boy. My hair was cropped short; I wore work boots, plaid flannel shirts and Levi's.

A catheter was inserted into my bladder. It felt like shards of glass were piercing me. Thick tubing was fed down my throat. I did not know that eventually it would suck all the green, slimy poison out of me.

The following day I woke up in the ICU revolted by the sight of the sludge being extracted from my stomach. After being moved to an upstairs room, people from the center, my dad, and my best friend, Sondra, came to visit.

It was in high school that Sondra and I discovered our love for one another. She was kind, gentle, smooth to the touch, and a fine kisser. I felt something with her I'd never felt with a boy. It was magical. It was electric. Deep and solid within me, I felt the passion for her. We never had any clear understanding of what was going on, but we knew our feelings had to be suppressed. We never pursued the physical part of our love further. Had homosexuality been an accepted form of love back then, perhaps we would have been high school sweethearts and gotten married. Now, here I was in the hospital with her again. Others had already sent cards asking why I would try to kill myself. I was afraid. I was ashamed. Would they stop loving me if they knew I was gay? I could not tell them.

After five days I was discharged from the hospital. I went back to the apartment. Marcia and Jen still lived there, and the women upstairs were asking about the day the ambulance came for me. I could see that I was not going to succeed in the psychiatric center's experiment and felt as though I was right back where I started in terms of accepting myself and becoming independent. So I left and went home to live with my father.

I tried to find information about being gay. I found no help at the library, and there was no Internet then, no educational websites for people like me who were considering suicide…not even a halfway decent role model to show me I was not alone. I could not accept heterosexuality as my lifestyle.

My sexual experiences were mostly with males—yes, I tried to fit into the heterosexual norm. I can't say those encounters were enjoyable or disgusting. They were casual, and the only satisfaction I felt was the closeness of being with another human body. I felt that heterosexuality was the only acceptable choice because I knew no other gay people, and the church rejected homosexuals. During my early 20's, my sexual experiences weren't temporary, uncaring or indiscriminate. But, at times, I regretted having sex with someone I didn't love.

With the exception of now-outdated drugs—Thorazine and Tofranil—prescribed by my psychiatrist, I dealt with my confusion and what had now become self-loathing by drinking. Three years following my attempt at suicide, I was nearly always in search of a drink.

I didn't know I was an alcoholic until I went to my first Twelve Step meeting at Doylestown Hospital. I was twenty-three and had decided there was no God. As I began to face my alcoholism in these meetings, I found my higher power, whom I now choose to call God. Society and other people had silenced me, but I felt God had listened. I attended the meeting, and that evening told my close friend, Nina, I wanted to quit drinking, and that there was a program that focused on a set of spiritual principles. All I had to do was to have the desire to stop drinking.

One night on the way home from my job as a school bus driver, I stopped at the liquor store and bought a bottle of Amaretto. I tooled around Newtown, where I worked, drinking from the bottle. I had never driven drunk up to that point. Hours later I got home to my dad's house in Levittown, puked on the shag carpet, and passed out on the floor.

I woke up at three o'clock in the morning, called my female sponsor, and told her I was in trouble. First, she chastised me for calling her after I drank, rather than before. Then she strongly recommended I get to a detoxification unit first thing in the morning. When Dad woke up, I told him what had happened and that I needed a ride to Warminster General Hospital. The ride was silent but felt right. Dad visited me often as I detoxed at Warminster General and later at Eagleville rehabilitation facility.

My parents had separated, and my mom had her set of problems and was living in turmoil. She was prescribed Valium by her primary care physician, and no one realized that she was allergic to it. It made her fly into fits of rage. Most times I was her target, making any relationship between us impossible.

The road to recovery was not easy. At one point, when things at Eagleville were especially tough, I reached my bottom, physically, spiritually, and emotionally. I felt I couldn't go on. I made a call to my dad, my strongest support then, pleading to be picked up.

"Dad, I just can't take it anymore. I want out of this place," I said.

"Go talk to your therapist. If you still want me to get you, I will," he said.

I could tell that he wanted me to stay and do the right thing, but he wasn't the type to push. My dad never raised his voice to me.

However, I was not a happy camper. I hated getting to group therapy by 6 a.m. There were times when extended therapy began at 8 p.m. and ran twelve hours! There were pillows placed around the room. Plastic bats propped up against walls stood ready to grab so we could beat the pillows and let out our pent-up rage. The idea was that we wouldn't be able to conceal our feelings either from ourselves or each other.

As a group, one of the tasks we performed was known as one-on-ones. Each member was expected to talk with the others in her group about her feelings and sense of progress in the program. When some of the women wanted to lie and say we had completed the one-on-ones when we hadn't, I was the one who told the staff the truth. I wanted to get sober. Honesty was important to me. I figured as long as I was being honest, it would be hard to pick up a drink.

I had been sober about a month when John Belushi died from a speedball—a combined injection of heroin and cocaine. The counselors gave us the news as though he were a member of our group. We fell silent. Gradually, people opened up to the tragedy of the event and talked about the insane things they had done out of desperation to satisfy their addiction.

The heroin addicts had the most to say. When there was no heroin, one guy shot whiskey into his veins because he wanted to get high. Another used orange soda in his syringe; another shot anti-freeze in an attempt to take his life. I did not want to wind up like Belushi or any of my group members. I wanted to live. I cried hard. Others silently stared into space. That day I chose sobriety. In that defining moment, I chose to believe that God had singled me out to succeed.

Over time in rehab, I began to accept myself in tiny steps. I learned that I needn't go it alone and gradually let God into my heart, my soul, and my mind. The hardest part was to admit that I had faith.

I called my dad to pick me up from rehab on an overcast and muggy July day in 1982. Before he got there, I walked to the beat-up dusty baseball diamond on Eagleville's campus. I could never hit a ball there for some reason. I sat on the field sobbing with no booze to ease the pain. Then I prayed.

"God, you know I drank every opportunity I got, so I wouldn't feel the pain. I know you want this for me, to live gay and to give up drinking. I only wish you could give me a sign...something to let me know that I am going to make it through this terrible time in my life."

Then I felt a presence around me. I opened my eyes and looked up. Light pierced the dark sky and clouds broke away and the sun shone, warming my face. The fog in my head began to dissipate. I could feel the depression lifting. I took long, deep breaths. I felt my prayers were heard.

I have been in an exclusive long-term relationship for thirteen years now. One of the things that concerns my partner and me is the concept of public displays of affection. I'm not speaking about the type of affection that has couples hanging all over one another. I'm merely referring to a peck on the lips at the airport, for example. Or greeting one another in the driveway after work and sharing a warm embrace. We are inclined to wait until we're in the house with the door closed before we hug or kiss.

I dream about the time when we can walk down the street holding hands and be accepted by society. Sadly, I feel that it's not likely to happen in my lifetime. But who knows? Maybe my prayers will be answered just as they were that day on what I now think of as the heavenly baseball diamond.

Steps — and Missteps — In the Right Direction

By KIMBERLY ELY

G avin adjusted his hair by sliding a long, curling thumb swiftly across his forehead at the spot just above the line of his glasses. He adjusted what were probably bangs once, though they were grown out now. He never adjusted his imposing tortoise shell glasses or his cherry-colored flannel shirt. The only thing that he bothered to touch at any point during class was his hair.

Gavin was polite enough to listen to instructions given at the start of class. At least he made it look like he was listening. When we broke into groups to complete assignments, Gavin remained in his seat, insisting he preferred to work alone. He never picked up his pencil. He never touched his binder. His hands quietly swept a few times over a set of ear-buds sitting in his backpack. He longed to wear them but could only sneak a gaze.

Standing in front of the room made me the teacher. I had waited four years for this, and then, there I was. I stared at the class and they stared back. I prayed to find the words to get through each lesson without sounding like a child repeating words I'd heard once in a book.

Meeting me at the front of the class each day was Gavin. He was a special species of enigma, a labyrinth of silent thoughts. I wondered constantly what he thought about the other kids in class, about school, or his life, or me. But he was a closed book, rarely saying anything at all.

My suit, pumps, and pearl necklace said, "I am in charge here; I am the professional in the room." My mother had gotten me the pearls as a wedding present. They were shiny and elegant. They were my first real grown-up gift, and I was determined to believe they possessed some ability to make me more mature. But they were like part of a costume that I couldn't quite pull off. The pearls sat beautifully, but I couldn't help adjusting them, fidgeting with them. I was sure when they looked at me, my students saw something less than a real teacher, a person with answers. The class saw someone who was nervous and unsure of herself. Kids can smell fear, or so I'd heard.

Thursday. I should have been taking attendance, but a wave of giggles started and distracted me. The students took turns reaching their arms back behind their heads to pantomime a throwing action. They were atypically focused and engaged.

First Dale had it. Then Joe. Then Steve. When Steve looked to Jessica for the pass, her eyes failed to meet his, and he inadvertently threw it to an empty space in the room. He received groans from a sea of classmates.

"You dropped it!" yelled Patrick. "You're out!" announced Tim. "It's not my fault if Jessica didn't catch it—she's out, not me!" Steve fought back.

I was unsure how to react. They successfully distracted themselves from schoolwork by *not* throwing a ball in class. I realized my job would never get any easier, and I wanted to play invisi-ball myself!

"Pick up the ball," Gavin told Jessica.

When Jessica motioned to grab the "ball" from the ground, I positioned myself across the room and made an interception. Game over.

"Time to get your books out, folks. Please turn to page 43 in your novel, *Speak*," I said.

Groans. Whines. Gavin smiles.

Friday. I cleared my throat to gain attention. The class settled. I started the students on their assignment and made my way to Gavin. I walked slightly on my toes to alleviate the ominous sound of my high heels on the tile flooring. I didn't want to sound authoritarian or imposing as I approached him.

"How is the assignment coming, Gavin?" I asked.

"Can't concentrate."

"Why is that?"

"I dunno. It's hard," he said, sweeping the eraser of his pencil across his binder.

"What can I do to help?"

"Nothing."

He paused. I raised a hand up to my neck to rub my pearls. Again, I struggled to find the right words to connect with this kid. I knew that "nothing" meant that he wanted me to do "something." It's typical teenager code. But I came up dry again, never finding the right words.

Then the bell rang, interrupting the fleeting moments of a first conversation between my silent friend and me. The class shuffled their usual shuffle and hurried out the classroom door. Gavin followed and quickly merged into a hallway of black backpacks, lost yet again.

Friday night.

I sat in a pile of three different quilts on our living room sofa. The colors swirled around me and I was safe, cuddled in the three-month knitting project of my favorite aunt. A mere three minutes has elapsed as I bite into my fourth double-stuffed Oreo cookie. Who the heck came up with the idea for these? I poked at my thighs, checking if I could feel the cellulite building.

What was so comforting and soothing about white crème and black crunch, anyway? Unfortunately, the comfort was temporary. I knew that a stomachache would surely follow because I never ate cookies. I never drank milk. I never indulged like this. So, a mixture of my guilt and the presence of unnatural, chemical-made foreign substances in my stomach were sure to lead to aching.

How do people eat to make themselves feel better? I felt worse almost instantly. I may have focused on my stomach for a short while, but the thoughts of school were still like spaniels incessantly nipping at my socks. *You feel terrible in your heart. And now you'll feel terrible in your stomach as well. Too bad for you*, I thought.

My mind drifted to my classroom. Gavin. Silent Gavin. I got into education to make a difference. I had my shot, standing there in front of the class. But, I didn't know what to do. I had frozen on the spot. I had become as silent as my student.

Over the last several months, as I started to come to grips with the fact that teaching high school English was probably not for me, the guilt of how much money my husband and I had spent on this dream of mine weighed me down.

Is $18,000 that much money? That's what we spent on coursework so that I could become a teacher. After the scholarships, the tuition remission, and the money from my parents, 18 grand came right out of our pockets. What could we have done with the money? What did we need it for? I remembered how we had talked about taking a needed vacation.

"Where do you want to go?" I had asked casually. "What do you want to see or feel or touch?"

My husband had paused for a minute, and I thought he was going to say something stupid like, "Let's go skinny dipping at the golf course pond."

Instead, he had looked at me wistfully and smiled.

"I want to go someplace where we will wake up to the clinking metal of a sailboat's mast against the rope pulleys."

It had been so romantic that I laughed uncomfortably. I tried to pretend it hadn't been the sweetest thing Matt had ever said.

When Matt got home from work, he instantly looked for the bag of Oreos in our pantry. Double Stuf were his favorite. When he noticed how many cookies were missing, he came and sat close to me on the couch.

"Are you cold?" he asked, looking at my colorful quilt.

I shrugged.

"How was your day?"

At that, I started to cry. I still couldn't find the words to explain things.

"I just don't know, Matt," I got out between sobs.

Matt rubbed my back and let me sniffle. He knew I wasn't ready to talk about it. He leaned in close to my nose, kissed me softly and said, "Do you want another Oreo? It's okay if you do."

Monday. The air had been still in the morning. Getting up was hard. I closed my eyes and wished for a snow day. I didn't want to be in the classroom anymore. I didn't want to be where I swore I didn't belong. Where I, still a child myself, couldn't fix anything.

Third period came. The class worked on their assignments without complaint. I was relieved. Gavin opened his binder to doodle on the inner flap. I wasn't eager to approach him. I pushed myself.

"Do you need help putting some ideas together?" I asked.

"I have ideas. I just can't concentrate."

"What can I do to help?"

Gavin's words spewed like a rusted pipe in a forgotten basement.

"I'm supposed to take my medicine. But I can't. Those drugs make me feel flat. Like I can't be happy or sad or anything. They make me skinnier when I take them because then I'm not hungry."

"Well, have you talked to your doctor? He can help you to find something different that may be able to help," I said.

Gavin thought about that. Then he said, "All those drugs that are supposed to make us work harder - they all have the same base chemicals. It's all the same stuff. No matter what I try, it won't make a difference," he insisted.

"The doctors don't care about us. They just give us whatever they want to," Sandra said across the room. "Last year, they told me I was bipolar. Now I have to eat pills every day. I'm going to be a pill-popper like my dad," she said, looking up through long brown lashes.

She hadn't looked at me all school year, and this was the first time I noticed stark blue eyes and the power of a fierce stare.

My heels froze in place while the students listened to each other. I didn't dare move to break the spell of their unleashed confession.

"You won't be like your dad. Just stop taking the pills like I did. I'd rather feel like crap than feel nothing at all. Those drugs make you feel numb," Gavin said.

It was the most Gavin had said all school year. I suddenly wished that I had gone to school to become a psychologist so that I could help these kids. Instead, all I could hear was the voice of a professor from graduate school in the back of my head saying, *Redirect student attention, reinforce the class objectives, keep students on track.*

But I ignored it. I just listened. And for once, everyone else in class did the same. They took turns, they spoke, and they nodded in agreement.

"No one cares about us. That's why we get so many Saturday detentions," Tim said.

"They don't even listen to our side of the story. When we get sent to the assistant principal's office, he's already heard from the teacher and has decided the punishment. He already has the detention slip filled out, already called home. We just sit in the office, tell two minutes of a story no one hears, and walk out with a Saturday detention," Patrick added.

I had known about Patrick's repeated detentions. He was the talk of the teacher's lounge with his so-called "problems with authority." To me, he was just a kid who asked a lot of questions. To the other teachers, he was a pain in the ass who got the class off track too easily.

"Sometimes, you're not going to get heard. This happens when you're a teenager as much as it does when you are an adult. Your boss may not listen to you. The dean at a college may not listen to you. A police officer may not listen to you," I told them.

"Then what are we supposed to do?" Gavin asked.

I thought for a minute, smiling to myself because this is what pedagogical books call *wait time*. It's meant to be an intentional pause in instruction to allow the kids enough time to think. But in that moment, I needed the time to think. I played with my wedding ring, twisting it around my finger. I reached up and rubbed my pearls. Then I looked up at the class of angry but teachable students.

"Well, it helps to become a better listener. It helps to hear what others have to say so that they will return the courtesy and listen to you. You also have to say things in the right way. That's why we're in school: to learn to articulate ourselves, to learn to write down our thoughts, and to learn how to be heard. The only downside is that learning these lessons takes time. In the process, we also learn how to be patient."

Everyone was silent for a long time. I wondered if I should redirect and ask the class to finish up their assignments. That's what my professor would have said, perhaps. But, I let the silence sit for a minute, suddenly unafraid of it. Then Gavin shifted through his backpack and produced an unspoiled, rarely used notebook. He began to fill in the boxes on the hall pass page. He swept hair behind his left ear and said, "Can I go to the nurse?"

I smiled, happy to grant him the access he had finally granted himself. I signed the slip, and reminded him to take his water bottle.

Monday night. I savored the feel of the sheets as I lay in bed. They knew how to become the perfect temperature. Those Egyptians must really know about thread count because I sat in a little bubble of heavenly sheets in my bed. I couldn't help but feel thankful for whoever actually invented Egyptian cotton.

Matt came up the stairs and flopped onto the bed.

"What's up? What are you thinking about?" he asked.

"Nothing. Just relaxing."

At first, I didn't want to get into the conversation. Silence had become my security blanket. But I thought of how brave Gavin had been, when he finally spoke up, and I searched for my own words.

I patted down Matt's rogue eyebrow. I looked at him, grateful for his endless support and kindness. He smelled good, and it put me at ease. Sweat, Men's Degree Deodorant, and rosemary.

Just say it, I told myself.

"I know that I said I wanted to go back to school to become a teacher."

I paused. Twisted my ring. Stared at my cuticles. Pulled a fuzzy piece of something out of the metal prong on my ring. Without looking at him, I said, "Matt, I just can't do this anymore."

His long fingers weaved their way through mine, and I took deep breaths, hoping that I could avoid crying.

"What is it that you don't like?" he asked.

"I feel like one of the kids. Lost and confused. Still trying to find myself. How can I teach them when I have no idea what I'm talking about?"

"You have every idea what you're talking about. You've read more books than anyone I know," Matt reminded me.

"Sure, I know about books. But these kids don't just need instruction on books. They are coming at me with their lives. They want guidance and help."

"Does that mean you want to be a guidance counselor instead?" he asked.

"No. I can't handle it. It's too much. When I cry at home, I'm not just crying for myself. I'm crying for them, too. I just don't have the personality to deal with what being a high school teacher really means," I explained.

I told him about the day I'd had, how I'd finally broken through to the kids and got them talking about their problems.

"That sounds amazing!" he said, proud of my accomplishment.

"But that's not what I was supposed to be doing. Getting them to talk and finally feel good about themselves was not in line with the curriculum. I spent time doing non-school stuff. And I can't say that I felt great about getting into all that stuff. I should be feeling amazing for touching their lives like that. But, I feel confused and still lost. I feel like I'm just not equipped for all this."

Matt stared, his hazel eyes slowly massaging my tender, raw feelings. Just talking to him made me feel better because I could let go of the voices circling in my mind.

And without skipping a beat he said, "So, what's next?"

When I heard the word *next* I suddenly realized that there could be a next. There was a next place to go. I didn't know what that would mean for me, but the spoken reminder that there could be a next somehow soothed me.

"I wish we had a school nurse here," I told him. He looked at me confused, but I knew what I meant; I had helped Gavin to speak up and get the access he needed to feel better. Now I would give myself permission to change and get better, too.

Matt kissed me softly and I breathed a sigh of relief. I had finally found the right words to explain how I felt. And that was the first step.

Why Women Stay

By Candice L. Swick

One of Trish's first "big" girl memories happened on a sunny Saturday afternoon when she had just turned eight years old. Her mom was hosting her monthly book club meeting and let Trish help make yogurt sauce for the cucumber sandwiches. Trish tried hard not to let the sauce seep out the sides of the bread. She was excited to help, and she had hopes that maybe, if she made the sauce right, next time she could make the whole sandwich. As Trish carefully placed the last sandwich on the white serving platter, she noticed her mother stopped stirring the iced tea.

"Trish honey, I know you're too young to understand right now, but I hope you'll remember what I'm about to tell you when you fall in love. The book the ladies and I are discussing today reminds me of something your grandmother told me, but I didn't listen. 'A woman needs to pay attention to a man's words, but even closer attention to his tone.' "

Trish licked the cucumber sauce off her pinky finger and shook her head with young girl confusion.

What did her mother mean? Trish wondered, *and why was she telling her this now?*

Fourteen years later — lying in her loft bed and dangling her dirty bare feet from the loft's edge — Trish found herself thinking about her mom's words. She knew she needed a shower. She was relying on the hot water to soothe her stomach.

The fight she had had with Tim earlier, after dinner, tied her stomach into knots. Her normal remedy for post-fight nerves — hiding under the covers — wasn't working this time. This time was different. This time Tim had become irrational and downright mean.

Her mom's remarks kept running through her brain. Trish thought, *Something tells me that there was a lesson in those words passed down from Grandma to Mom to me.* She couldn't remember the exact words, but she was determined to figure out what the lesson was.

The small one-room efficiency apartment, their quaint little love haven, started to look more and more like a large punishment closet. *It's going to be a long night,* Trish thought. *He's probably not even that upset. I bet he's grabbing a drink with friends, and here I am crying like a lovesick puppy. What's wrong with me?*

After their screaming match, Tim did what he did best. He left. Things got hot, and he couldn't stand the heat. He grabbed his dingy gray jean jacket and slammed the door, bam! Summer sweat trickled down Trish's cheek mixing with a full hour's worth of a 22-year-old young woman's tears as she relived this most recent episode.

"You're a controlling bitch and I'm done. I'm not budging on this one Trish; it's not debatable. I'm following my gut this time and I'm doing my solar capsule with or without you. Don't worry I'm not asking for any of your parents' money. If you really loved me you'd support me, but if you can't then you should just get out."

As Tim slammed drawers and rummaged through papers, Trish moved into the corner of the loft. She saw hate deepen in his eyes, and her fear of him grew. Finding what he was looking for, he started waving papers up at her.

"See look, it's only my name on the lease. You don't owe me anything, so you can just leave. Get your shit and run home to Mommy and Daddy."

Tim's face, red and sweaty, started to reveal a meanness she wasn't able to confront. She couldn't believe his anger about this solar capsule invention. While Tim yelled and moved his hands in the air, Trish thought, *He can't really be this mad can he? In the whole two years we've been together, he's never hollered at me with his marine voice. Were these words coming from the same guy, who just last Tuesday fed me grapes while I read Sylvia Plath for my creative writing class?*

As 10 p.m. approached, Trish wondered where Tim had gone… if he would be coming home. Her fiancé seemed to enjoy messing up her happy little tinker-toy playhouse. Feeling confused and worn out, Trish's usual common sense insight couldn't wrap itself around Tim's verbal eruption. His anger made no sense to her. She knew that he was passionate about his invention, but when they first discussed it, he seemed on board with waiting until the timing was better. She thought they agreed that saving for their wedding would come first.

Her head pounded as she climbed down the steps of the loft. Leaving her cozy, fetal position made her feel vulnerable and exposed.

Trish made her way into the tiny bathroom and looked in the mirror trying to convince herself that everything was okay. Without realizing it, she subconsciously started counting the bathroom faucet drips. One, now what? Two, right is right. Three, but this is all wrong. Four, fine — let me just start from the beginning again.

Tim wants to marry me. He loves me. He needs me. He's just confused right now. After he cools off, he'll come to his senses. He can't be serious about this dumb invention. No one wants to heat their pool with an ugly solar capsule that probably doesn't even work. We're supposed to be saving for our wedding, not for a patent. Wrong, wrong, wrong. This is all wrong.

———◦———

Suddenly, it was 2012 and she found herself alone, remembering that horrible night thirteen years ago. As she sat in the diner and stirred creamer into her decaf coffee, Trish heard the waitress ask, "What can I get ya, sweetie? How 'bout I bring you the special, a hot turkey sandwich with gravy and mashed potatoes. Sound good?"

Lost in the haze of her memories, Trish ordered a bagel and forced herself to eat.

Not realizing how long she had been in the diner, she checked the time on her cell phone. *I should have left ten minutes ago. Way to go, late again.* She told herself to relax. *Breathe in, breathe out, breathe in, breathe out. Calm down.* She needed to calm down before driving to her bi-weekly therapy session.

Divorced, I'm divorced and better off. Trish repeated her "safe," soothing words as she grabbed the third Kleenex of the session. Nicki, her counselor, reassured her that eventually she would believe those words, but for now she should just keep repeating them for comfort. Soon she would be confident in her decision.

Driving home from her session, Trish replayed that first big fight with Tim about his invention and asked herself, *why did I stay when it wasn't right so early in our relationship?*

Then she remembered that summer day when she was eight…when she walked in and glanced in on the end of her mom's monthly book club meeting.

The woman in the red hat asked the other ladies if they would mind her reading the poem at the end of the book. The women said, "Of course not!" as they poured more wine. They listened to her read:

No, really he's not that mean
I only tell you the bad stuff.
There's lots of good in between.

My job pays too little to leave
So I keep rolling up my sleeves.
I dig deeper to show him I care
Then my heartstrings begin to tear.

He doesn't mean to lie
When he looks me in the eye.
We've been together forever
Really, he's a good guy.

Like I said, it's not that bad
It's not like he cheats.
He can't help it
if he gets mad.

He doesn't hit
He just demeans
A little bit.
I shouldn't complain
It's not real pain.

I can't leave.
Where would I go?
The kids need their dad.
No. Things will get better.
He's not that bad.

Eight-year-old Trish waited until the lady finished reading before walking into the living room. She handed her mom the second tray of cucumber sandwiches. As she took the tray, Trish's mom looked her in the eye and said,

"That, my dear, is why women stay."

An older, wiser Trish gripped the steering wheel. Confidently she said aloud, "Divorced, I'm divorced. I'm better off that I didn't stay."

Motherhood

Stepping Stone House

By Susan G. Weidener

❧

"What do you think, darling?" her husband asked.

"A sensible investment," she said. "Good neighborhood and school district. Move on in a couple years to a bigger place." *A stepping stone house,* she thought.

A solitary maple tree captured Claire's attention, as they stood on the front lawn. Bare of all but a few gold leaves, it looked young and new like the house, which was only two years old. The realtor described it as a New England saltbox which made sense because of its boxy shape, no shutters, cedar siding. Claire and Mark hugged. That night they bid on the property. The house on Maplewood Drive was theirs.

As soon as they moved in, their six-year-old son Brett jumped up and down on his bed while Mark put up a colorful poster of stegosaurus, tyrannosaurus rex, and triceratops wandering an arid landscape.

Four-year-old James ran into his bedroom with a view of the maple tree. He carefully spread his little brown bear rug at the foot of the bed.

Claire loved the master bedroom. The wallpaper was lilacs and day lilies set against a pure white background. The curtains matched, so Claire had paid extra at settlement to buy them from the previous owners. In that bedroom, it felt as if she and her husband were sleeping in a garden. When Mark made love to her the first time in their new home, she looked deep into his dark eyes and he into her green ones as he slowly moved on top of her.

Afterwards, they showered in the small master bath. He lathered her body with vanilla-scented soap, his hands slowly moving inside her legs and up again. They kissed long deep kisses as the water cascaded on their heads. She loved the way the hair on his arms and chest looked as the water ran it into dark rivulets.

That first summer, 1989, she and Mark invited her parents over for drinks and dinner to enjoy the new wood deck Mark had built. The Pennsylvania air felt warm and dry, no hint of humidity, making for a perfect June evening as they sat outside. The liquor flowed as they talked — her parents enjoyed drinking!

Her father scoffed when he heard they had bought a desktop computer and set it up in the fourth bedroom. Wouldn't waste space or money on one of those, said the man whose complete collection of Shakespeare, Donne, and Hawthorne had graced the bookshelves of Claire's childhood home. Mark explained without sounding challenging that technology was the wave of the future and it would be good for the boys to feel comfortable around computers.

Teddy, their blond cocker spaniel, sprawled on the deck against her mother's high-heeled feet. Her mother surreptitiously slipped the dog a piece of cheese, although Claire had warned her it could make Teddy sick. *So what if her mother never listened? This is all that matters in life,* Claire thought. *Family. Even if they are half drunk.*

As the afternoon slowly slipped into dusk, Brett and James raced down to the finished basement where video games mesmerized them for hours. When Claire brought her sons pizza and soda on a tray, she was reminded of little robots. Their eyes were glued to the television screen, their fingers feverishly working controls that moved futuristic-looking men and women in armor, wielding shields and swords. Upstairs, she heard the pop of a champagne cork and her mother's laugh like a soprano trilling an aria.

By the end of the evening, Claire felt tired and content as she and Mark walked her parents down the narrow foyer and then closed the front door behind them. *A handsome, smart husband and two attractive little boys. A lovely new home. What more could a woman want,* she thought?

But she should have known nothing lasts forever; the fragile promise of tomorrow was broken in an instant after one medical visit and horrifying test results.

"I'm sorry, babe," he whispered, tears in his eyes.

Toward the end, after exhausting every search for a cure, she and Mark spent many nights in the small fourth bedroom that was used as a combination study/computer room. Mark slept on the white sofa in that room. Sleeping together in the same bed had become impossible because he was in so much pain. Bottles and vials of morphine and other drugs were lined up like soldiers on the mahogany night table to fight an enemy that showed no mercy. It was here on the white sofa that they would reminisce about their sixteen years together — all that was and all that could have been, but never would be.

After her husband died, the first thing Claire did was haul the white sofa curbside to be thrown away by the trash men. She had also made another decision: She would keep the house on Maplewood Drive. The boys had friends here on this tree-lined cul-de-sac where in the summers children sold lemonade and played basketball and street hockey. Keeping the house would also help maintain normalcy amidst the devastation she now confronted; she was a widow at the age of forty-three and a mother to two boys who had just turned eleven and nine.

Keeping the house went against the well-meaning advice of friends. "Sell," they all chorused. "You don't need the lawn maintenance or repairs."

Would they be saying the same if she were a man? She doubted it. Besides, where would she go? An apartment? A townhouse? The thought repelled her because it meant losing the big backyard, and her privacy, which she felt she desperately needed if she were to carry on.

Widow and *single mother* duly evoked all the horrors that came with those labels, at least if you believed what you read or saw in the news. Women struggling to make ends meet, women fearful of being alone and trying to do it all, who speedily remarried an inappropriate partner only to learn he didn't get along with her children or they with him. Worst of all were the predators who betrayed your trust and stole your money.

Claire was angry. She had lost her faith in happy endings. Nor had she bargained for having to be mother and father, nurturer and disciplinarian, and dealing with every crisis from failing hot water heaters to poor grades on report cards! But along with her anger, her determination grew and took root that her sons would have everything many children with two parents took for granted, including a single family home.

She fought like a lioness for her children. The man next door angrily approached her one night as she watered the pink and red impatiens she had planted near her front walkway. Without preamble, he said his wife told him that when Claire's children got home from school, they had been kicking a soccer ball and running across his lawn. He wanted it to stop. She felt a gorge of anger rise in her throat. He and his wife had avoided her since Mark's death. Maybe the wife worried that the same fate could happen to her, although Claire could almost hear her spitting out the words *latch key kids* like an epitaph. The thing was, Claire worked

20 minutes down the road and Brett, at eleven years old, was smart and knew what to do in an emergency. Claire also had a high school girl stay with the boys until she got home from work, something Brett resented, insisting he was old enough to watch his brother. The girl had called that week to say she was sick and couldn't watch the boys, so Claire had risked leaving them alone.

She looked at the man with his shaved blond head and icy blue eyes. "I forgot your grass was paved in gold," she said with chilly sarcasm.

She felt relief when he turned on heel and walked away. Good. That would teach him. She felt the protective shell she had begun to develop growing harder, sharper.

Her kitchen with its large greenhouse window and southern exposure helped comfort her during those early weeks and months of loss. It was hard to be depressed, at least in the mornings when the sun shown in all its radiance on the white ceramic floors and the tawny butcher block table. But oh how she missed those commonplace conversations over coffee with her husband, at the same time feeling rising panic because they were receding, becoming more and more distant and vague. It seemed the emotions remained as strong as ever even as the details faded. To prevent it from all slipping away, she sat alone at night in her bedroom and began keeping a journal, a reporter's spiral notebook, because what she did for a living was report other people's stories. But she had never thought she would be writing her own.

Sometimes she felt his presence, a whisper of wind in the backyard when she put Teddy outside and stood on the deck. "Are you out there?" she murmured. A soft breeze like fingertips lightly caressed her cheek.

Huge silhouettes from the black walnut trees slanted across the back lawn in the moonlight as the dog barked and sniffed. The trees had once formed the barrier line to break wind and rain on the old farm on which their subdivision of thirty homes had been built. She didn't know when she and Mark bought the house that nothing grows near black walnut trees. Not flowers, not vegetables; something in the tree poisons the soil around it.

She called Teddy and went back inside the house. She wouldn't allow everything else in her life to be poisoned because of cancer.

Two years passed before she brought a man upstairs to the flowered bedroom. She thought – no, she wanted to believe – she was in love, if for no other reason than she desperately missed the touch of another human being holding her close. Afterwards, she felt a rush of guilt along with the sinking sensation that it wasn't love as much as thirst and she had fallen for a mirage. Had Mark been watching? In her heart, she was still Mark's wife. She always would be. But she had to move on. Isn't that what everyone kept insisting she do? She had heard it so many times she wanted to scream. Still, she knew they were right. She tried hard, but moving on when it came to love – like moving out of the house – eluded her.

Late at night after the boys were asleep, she sat in the living room staring at pictures on the wall. The boys, posed with their backs leaning against each other like bookends, looked solemnly into the camera. She in white wedding gown and he in cream-colored tux standing before the big red oak door of the Episcopal Church. Her parents on an Easter Sunday long in the past: Dad in coat and tie, wearing a hat he had bought in Switzerland with bird feathers tucked in the brim; Mother in a bright red coat with stylish gold buttons.

Claire's father had died of prostate cancer seven months after her husband had died. Claire's mother struggled with dementia, and Claire had become her power-of-attorney and moved her into assisted living. Her mother had become another child. Now she had three children to care for; the boys and her mother. *Its classic*, Claire thought with grim irony. *Woman as caretaker. Do we ever escape the role?*

Yet it felt comforting to look at all those pictures of days gone by. The house held so many memories! The people she loved and lost had walked these rooms, laughed over wine, studied themselves in the gilt mirror above her upright piano.

This house held her life. It spoke of her independence as a single mother and as a widow. She had begun to accept both as describing who she was and hold them as badges of honor. It was nothing to be ashamed of; rather, it spoke of her determination to live a life as true to herself as she could.

Upstairs, her sons slept soundly, the dinosaur poster long ago replaced by posters of Kurt Cobain and the Beatles on the cover of "Abbey Road"; the bear rug thrown to the back of the closet because blankets and pillows with a Philadelphia Eagles logo now dominated.

One day, one step at a time, she had slowly found her rhythm in the house, making dinner when she got home from the office, helping the boys with homework and then settling into the plush pink bedroom chair to write in her journal. The wolf was not knocking at the door. She had a job, some money – not a lot – but enough. Most of all, she had her own nest, her space, her private place to shut out the world and its realities, its horror and fear. A place to rest, close her eyes and dream again that maybe something wonderful might come her way when she least expected it.

She and her children were thriving like the maple tree that had grown tall and sturdy since that day when he looked at her and asked, "What do you think, darling?"

The Last to Know

By Diane Yannick

Annie, Laura, and Rob gathered around my cluttered, crayon marked kitchen table. Longtime friends and colleagues at the rural middle school where I taught English, they had decided to surprise me with an impromptu birthday celebration. A bottle of Thunderbird wine, our frugal favorite, and a lopsided angel food cake, complete with a few mismatched candles, were presented with exaggerated finesse.

"Happy Birthday, dear Diane! Happy Birthday to you!" they sang.

Amid laughter and hugs, I swiped my finger into the icing puddled around the base of my cake. Yum!

I quickly blew out the candles, closed my eyes and made a heartfelt wish for a healthy new year. It was January 23, 1976. I was twenty-eight years old. I had no inkling what my new year would hold.

As they cut the cake into oversized hunks, I took a minute to reflect. My life wasn't perfect, but it felt okay. I knew that I had lots to celebrate.

My husband, Kirk, had recently landed a job teaching elementary music at a school near my middle school. We had bought our first house in rural Delaware. It wasn't fancy, but we loved it. Best of all, I was positively sure there had never been a child quite as smart or beautiful as our two-year-old daughter, Christy. My feet wanted to do a happy dance every time I looked at her.

While I was continually amazed by our precious daughter's every little accomplishment, Kirk seemed immune to her charms. He chose not to enter into her toddler world of make believe. He saved his passion for hunting, fishing, farming, and riding motorcycles. I was disappointed that he spent so much time away from home. Promises to spend more time as a family were seldom kept.

"Diane," Annie prodded. "Aren't you going to eat this cake that I slaved over?"

Clearing my head, I smiled and grabbed for the chipped plate holding my hunk of cake.

"Where's Kirk? How come he isn't here?" Annie asked.

"He's hunting," I responded with a casual sweep of my hand.

"What's he hunting?"

"Ducks, I think, maybe pheasant." It was hard to keep track of what was in season. "He'll be back a little later."

Annie persisted. "Diane, it's dark out. How do you hunt in the dark? Are you sure he's hunting?"

"Well, yeah. That's what he said. I think he has a duck blind in Maryland. It takes a while to drive there. Maybe that duck blind is in Smyrna." I realized I wasn't positive where he was.

Making excuses for Kirk's absences made me uncomfortable even though I'd had plenty of practice. When all three of them continued to stare at me, I headed for the sink and started to wash some left over dirty breakfast dishes. I tried to lighten the mood by swatting at them with my dishtowel. "Come on, let's dance or something!"

They continued to stare, but now they were fidgety, too. They seemed to be speaking some kind of silent, secret language. "Hey, did you guys buy me a present?" I teased.

They quickly cleared the kitchen table and motioned for me to sit. I wondered if I'd lost my job or if one of them had a fatal disease.

"Guys, you're scaring me. What's going on?"

Annie broke the silence. "How are you and Kirk getting along?"

Why was she asking me this silly question? She was my best friend. We shared everything. I studied her face. A pained expression furrowed her brow. I consciously slowed my breathing. I knew I had to say something. "Well, he's gone a lot, like you know. Sometimes it's late when he gets home. We're fine. He's thrilled with his new motorcycle. I'm not too thrilled with our finances, but we both have jobs. He's president of the teacher's union this year. They have many meetings. It's a contract year." I had to quit rambling. Was I even making sense?

Rob spoke in a hushed voice, "Diane, he is not always at meetings or hunting when he's gone." The others solemnly nodded in agreement.

I'd had it with this slow-paced game of words. "What in the hell are you guys trying to say?" I demanded, rising from the chair.

"We're trying to say," Annie began, "We're trying to say that . . .."

"Kirk is seeing Sandra," Rob blurted out.

I dropped back into the kitchen chair. Was this some kind of cruel joke?

"You guys are crazy," I heard myself shouting. "Sandra is one of my best friends. Do you know what you're saying? She has a husband and I teach next door to him!"

I listened with disbelief as they described the ongoing affair between my husband and one of my best friends. With my silence and nods, I allowed them to relay the lurid details of my now-mangled marriage. It seems that my til-death-do-us-partner had been sneaking around for months, maybe even a year. When I thought he was on union trips and hunting forays, he was shacking up with Sandra.

My friends stayed for another hour while I intermittently sobbed, cursed, paced, and seethed. Laura, a lady of few words, gave her parting advice. "That bastard never did deserve you. Do not let him bring you down."

I nodded numbly.

"I love you," Annie said tearfully. "Call any time and I'll be there. Okay, Dee? You're going to be fine."

Rob, my big teddy bear of a friend, gave me a big hug and whispered in my ear. "We had to tell you. Sorry it was on your birthday but there were rumors floating around school. We were afraid you would find out really soon."

Then they were gone. I numbly watched them drive away. So much for my birthday celebration.

I truly was the proverbial last to know. I felt like a fool. All I could hear or think were the four words: *Kirk is seeing Sandra.*

I watched their cars until they disappeared from view. Then I watched some more. I trembled, my head spinning, my hands perspiring. Finally I glanced at the kitchen clock. Ten p.m. It was several hours later than the time Rich said he planned to be back. The stark light from the ceiling fixture cast my shadow on the wall as I paced the uneven linoleum floor. *Had I become immune to his empty promises? Had I purposely ignored clues? What were the clues?* I urged myself to keep moving . . . not to think.

I walked into Christy's bedroom and watched the rhythm of her sleeping breaths. I put my hand on her back to ground myself. Forcing myself to recall happy times, I pictured her digging in the summer sand, squealing with joy as a sand crab wriggled onto her plastic shovel. I saw Baby Robin, her favorite doll tucked beside her. They had matching, carefully hand sewn pjs. I kissed them both lightly on the tops of their heads.

Then I went to the back of the house and turned on the light in the laundry room. I methodically folded my husband's tee shirts while

I searched for cracks in the stories I'd heard that night. I pleaded with God, *Please don't let this be true. I'll never ask for anything else, God.* Tears burned my cheeks. Ebony, my much loved stray cat who had come to my door a few years ago and never left, rubbed against my leg. I bent down to pat him realizing that I'd forgotten to feed him. Wishing all problems could be so easily solved, I poured his food into the bowl.

I headed back to the kitchen and turned off the light. I could see my beat-up Ford Pinto in the unpaved driveway next to Kirk's rusty John Deere tractors. To my surprise, he unexpectedly announced one day that he wanted to farm even though we only had a small yard and he would need to rent land to farm. On his insistence we had taken a trip to Tennessee so that he could arrange to have his uncle's old tractor shipped to us. We absolutely couldn't afford to do this, but we did. He wouldn't have it any other way. Now, another of his impulsive ideas sat there in the yard staring at me. I glared at that broken tractor and the tall grass growing up through the cultivators. Then I forced myself to look away.

I counted to one hundred forward and then backwards, a childhood ritual I had used to block out arguments between my mom and dad. Finally I just stood staring out the kitchen window until my legs ached and my tears dried.

The lights from his pickup truck startled me as he pulled into the driveway. As he opened the door, I heard him humming the theme song to "Star Wars," his favorite movie.

"Oh, you waited up for me. I'm really hungry. Is there anything left?"

I watched in disbelief as he cut himself a piece of my lopsided birthday cake. "Do not eat that cake," I said with calculated calmness.

"Why?" he countered with a whine. "I'm hungry, for heaven's sake."

"Where have you been tonight?" I asked, amazed at how calm I sounded.

"What's this, the grand inquisition? I told you that I was going to Sean's duck blind in…."

"Where were you really?" I cut him off in a monotone.

"Hey, look, I've had a long day. Can't we talk about this tomorrow?"

He was becoming agitated. I studied him carefully. It was then that I knew for sure that my prayers would go unanswered.

"You cheating, no good, sorry excuse for a husband! You and Sandra? My friends have seen you with her! You sneaking...." My voice broke.

"Wh—who—what?" Kirk stammered looking around the room, any place but at me, his wife of seven years.

I waited for his denial. Only silence.

"What do you want me to say?" he asked quietly.

"I want you to tell the truth," I said just as quietly.

"Well, the truth is that I have been seeing Sandra."

His eyes averted mine. I watched as his mouth hardened and his expression changed from surprise to defiance.

"Do you love her?" I held my breath.

"Well, you know we've been having some problems lately. You spend more and more time with Christy and you don't...."

I tuned out the rest. "Do you love her?"

"Yes."

"Have you had sex with her?" I continued, not sure why this mattered.

"Yes," he said looking out the window into the murky blackness of the night.

I leaped up, ran to our bed and buried my face in the pillow to muffle my sobs. There was absolutely no way to make this right, even if he had wanted to. Shattered, I shut my eyes as adulterous images pummeled my eyelids. If I slept, in the morning I'd have to convince myself again that this was not a nightmare. I lay there as still as I could until daybreak. My marriage was over.

In the days that followed, Kirk moved out of our house. At first, I hated myself for not being what he wanted. I blamed myself just like I always had as a child when my father had bullied me. Gradually, my life came into clearer focus. *What about him? What about Kirk and his responsibility to me to be a good husband and father?*

He was the one who spent so much money on stereo equipment, hunting, fishing, motorcycles, and tractors that we often couldn't pay our bills. Still not satisfied, he had recently started lobbying for his own boat and he was still looking for land to farm. I took after-school tutoring jobs to make extra money.

He was the one who stayed up late and couldn't get to work on time. Put on probation for being late too many times, he was in danger of losing his job.

I had to quit playing this game of blame. I had to move forward. We talked about the house, our possessions, our daughter. Each discussion was laden with tainted memories and unbearable pain. After a time, we talked only when necessary. I busied myself with the details of life, the more mundane the better.

I felt overwhelmed by teaching and mothering. I felt embarrassed, not knowing what to say to Sandra's husband, my colleague. I wanted to move away and start again where no one knew me. Mostly, I wished that I could just hide under the covers and never come out.

On my lowest days, I invented scenarios for Kirk and Sandra. I wished they would get struck by lightning, eat a mad cow burger, get decapitated by a low flying helicopter, or sink slowly and completely into welcoming mucky quicksand.

Unfortunately, Delaware had no mad cows or quicksand, so I had to push forward without revenge. I cried over the big things and the little things. Who would get the rocking chair that I had saved green stamps to buy? Who would tell his grandparents, whom I adored? Would I get to keep our beloved Chihuahua? Did I even know how to start the finicky old lawn mower?

I reminded myself of my childhood mantra, *You can do this, Diane.* I muddled through life on automatic pilot. Every day I taught my English classes. Every night I made lesson plans and graded papers. I did every-thing I possibly could to make Christy happy. I knew how to do that. I understood what a child needed. My childhood held many hard lessons. I had spent way too much time blaming myself for things that were not my fault. I was almost finished feeling that I was not good enough.

The day I signed my final divorce papers, I stopped on impulse at the Volkswagen dealership. I saw a shiny red VW bug sitting in the showroom. I needed that car. More importantly, I felt I deserved that car. A few short hours later, I drove away in my first new car. I was not at all sure what I was celebrating, or what direction I was headed, but I felt myself smile.

Shriver's Bench: Or, Why Women Leave

By Candice L. Swick

Somewhere in the fifteen years with Tim and Robby, Trish forgot about herself. As she focused on the central needs and requirements of her husband and his son, she conveniently tucked herself away like an old rabbit's foot hidden in a memory box. Nobody noticed she went missing.

I need to stop feeling guilty. Robby and Tim will be fine without me this weekend, she thought as she kept walking. *There's frozen turkey lasagna in the freezer and Robby's going to a friend's house for the weekend, so Tim doesn't have anything to be pissed off about.*

Meanwhile, the salty ocean breezes skipped atop the waves stirring up white foam. Trish walked the familiar Ocean City, New Jersey, boardwalk, and kept trying to convince herself that spending a weekend, alone, to think clearly without distractions, would prove a good thing. *Like a post-traumatic stress disorder victim*, she kept repeating to herself,

This isn't my real decision, not my final one. I just need to quiet my mind. I need a second to actually think about myself and what I need, not what I want, but what I need to be okay.

Trish was so lost in her thoughts that she was almost run over by a big surrey bike. She stepped out of the way just in time as a snotty teenage boy yelled,

"God lady! Get the hell out of the bike lane!"

The boy's hair was light brown, long, and greasy. It reminded Trish of the countless hygiene battles she had recently fought with Robby. Getting him to do anything without a major argument had become impossible. As much as it pained Trish to admit, she knew that if she decided to leave she'd miss those petty arguments.

She needed to stop thinking that her marriage was over. The sense of finality sent shivers of fear down her spine. Trish felt a moment of relief when she saw Shriver's Saltwater Taffy Shop coming up at the next block. *Ah, saved again by chocolate fudge,* she thought.

As she got closer, Trish saw Mr. Peanut shaking the kids' hands outside the store. The image of the self-confident Peanut Man swept her back in time to 2001.

———○———

Robby was only seven then, and he was crying. The melting chocolate cone with the rainbow jimmies had ruined his favorite "Buzz Light Year" shirt. Trish remembered how he loved that grey shirt with its red glow-in-the-dark letters. Trying to calm Robby down, Trish promised him as many rides and staying up as late as he wanted. Trying to salvage Robby's shirt by dabbing water on the stain, Trish looked up to ask Tim for another napkin, but he wasn't there. He was leaning over the railing looking out at the ocean, having one of his far-off moments.

He's never been there when I really need him, Trish thought.

She had seen that look many times when he cut her out from wherever his distracted thinking led.

It's so weird how he just turns off all of a sudden.

She first noticed Tim's detachment in the early days of dating, but it never caused any real problems. Back then Robby visited only every other weekend. But now when Tim zoned out, Trish had to take charge. Robby needed a parent, and it seemed like Tim wasn't up to the job.

———————

Now, sitting on the bench outside of Shriver's, Trish thought about the events of that 2001 beach trip and somehow realized they reminded her of a B-rated movie. Girl loves boy. Boy suddenly becomes a stranger... and a nasty stranger at that.

"Trish, when the hell did buying amusement ride tickets become such a huge ordeal? I've been standing in line for fifteen minutes and now when it's my turn, I have to figure out what package to buy?"

Trish and Robby had been coming back from the bathroom, and Tim was in line for tickets. Trish took one look at his face and remembered thinking, *What's wrong now?* She didn't have long to wait for the blast of his words to hit her.

"Really! Come on now! This is ridiculous. Since these beach memories are for your dumbass scrapbook, you figure it out. I'm done. I can't handle this commotion. Do whatever you want; you always do any way."

———————

Sitting on the bench, Trish cringes in pain for the woman she is now, the woman who realizes her marriage is over, and soon she will be alone. She aches for her naïve self, the one who was raising a man's son; yet, that man blamed her for everything. Still...maybe if she could just turn back the clock and forget all of this? *No. Impossible.*

Why hadn't she left him yet? Somehow while she was living "it", none of "it" seemed *that bad. They would fight, but no matter how hard she tried, Trish couldn't stay mad at him. They had fallen into a repetitive cycle. They would fight about money, or raising Robby, or Tim lying about spending money. His lying to avoid conflict hurt Trish the most. She constantly felt betrayed, but Tim was one hell of a sweet talker. He knew exactly how to get her into bed. Before she knew it, everything would be better again. She would be back on autopilot. She had a mission to raise a little boy and keep an emotionally chaotic man at peace. How did I keep it together for so long?* Pushing aside the nagging question, Trish allowed her mind's eye to revisit that scene nine years ago outside the board-walk amusement park.

——◦——

Standing in line, Robby's cotton-candied fingers are linked tightly in hers. He's rocking anxiously from his left foot to his right foot, left to right, and just before he's ready to burst with excitement, the ride attendant calls,

"Tickets! Tickets please! That'll be three tickets to ride the Brazen, Blazin' Cars!"

Robby looks up at Trish with pure joy and says, "As soon as that gate opens I'm getting the blue car. I know it's the fastest. I watched and the last kid who rode the blue one got the most bumps and he was smiling the biggest. Yup, I want the blue car; the red one's too slow."

The wholesome excitement and anticipation showed in Robby's little-boy eyes. The green chain gate opened and that blue car was all Robby's. Trish felt the fresh sea air on her cheek, smelled caramel corn, and saw Robby's wide grin as he whipped around in his blue bumper car. She loved seeing him happy. Robby had been through so much with his mom and abusive stepdad, and he finally seemed settled in with some of the carefree spirit a child should have. Trish felt a sense of pride in raising her stepson.

Physically, Tim stood right next to her watching his son have the time of his life, but he couldn't have been more emotionally disconnected. Trish knew without even looking that Tim was fiddling with his pocketknife. Usually, when he got that removed look in his eyes, he would be opening and closing each attachment of his knife.

———◦———

The summer of 1995: Wearing cut-off jean shorts, Birkenstocks and a clear crystal necklace, Trish held onto Tim like she'd never let go. The Ferris wheel stopped to let the next couple on, and Tim stared at her with hungry desire.

"Stop it, stop staring at me. I hate when you do that."

"I can't help it. I could stare at your blue eyes and cherry red lips all day, and you know you love it."

And she did. Trish loved the way he would stop whatever he was doing when she least expected it and stare at her. She was his Miss America, his beauty queen. The intensity of his deep brown eyes both thrilled and scared her. Tim was her first real love, and she fell hard and fast. His smooth muscled chest and broad shoulders were sexy and protective. Tim worked construction. He was rugged and, as her mom would say, "rough around the edges." His seductive animal maleness made her feel small and in need of protection. She couldn't explain it, but she liked the intoxication she felt.

After the Ferris wheel ride, Tim forced her to go on the haunted house ride. It wasn't her thing, but fair was fair. Trish remembered leaning against the wooden wall of the boardwalk haunted house. Her skin was hot and tingly, and it wasn't sunburn hot, but young love hot. Tim was leaning in, stopped briefly to brush back a piece of her blond hair. His calloused fingers touched her cheek sending chills through her body. It was taking him forever, and she could smell the mixture of his suntan lotion and Drakkar cologne. He was driving her crazy. She was electric for him, and when his lips finally sank into hers, she let herself go with him completely. That was the night she fell in love with Tim. Wherever he was going, she was going too.

In 1995 Trish was still in college and caught up in her studies. There wasn't time to overanalyze her new boyfriend. All she had room for was the fun: the ignited romantic side of Tim. Him nibbling on her ear while they watched a movie; Tim giving her an impromptu shoulder massage.

The euphoric magnetism between them blindfolded her and covered up anything bad. He made her feel fresh and alive, and she was his — all his.

It didn't matter that he had a two-year-old son from a previous relationship, or that he was bankrupt. Tim's attentiveness seemed to cancel out any negatives about his personality.

Her mind liked that young love movie. Trish replayed the memories of their romance with nostalgia and longing. Whenever Trish allowed her heart to steer, she felt like a teenager listening to her favorite song over and over again. Sadly, she no longer felt much comfort from the memories. Like the old music tapes, she was exhausted.

———◆———

The sun beat down on Trish's bare shoulders as she came back to the present. Like the tides, Trish's moods ebbed and flowed. For the last two years, there had been another person in her marriage, a cyber-person, and Trish was sick of feeling like the third wheel. Tim's late nights on the Internet with his Facebook friends were hurting their marriage.

Tim's earlier dream of inventing the great solar capsule that never came to pass had recently been replaced by becoming a world famous screenwriter. She tried to support him by encouraging him to take a film class, but he accused her of not believing in him. According to his Facebook family, he didn't need any classes; they were a waste of time. He should just go for it. Her husband was slowly being seduced right before her eyes, and Trish couldn't do anything about it.

Tim refused counseling. Trish begged him to fight for her and Robby. She tried enticing him with glorious memories; she reminded him of the nights when one of them would get the other's toothbrush because the other was too lazy to get out of bed. And she asked him to remember those long ago mornings when waking up was all about sharing each other's dreams in full Technicolor detail. They used to brainstorm about putting that pool-hot tub combo right out back; they'd plant some semi-dwarf cherry trees to create a secluded get away right in their own backyard.

Nothing seemed to break through Tim's fantasy world of becoming the next great Aaron Sorkin or Steven Spielberg. He wasn't content with just being himself. Worst of all; he wasn't content with her anymore.

The night before Trish left for the shore, she was standing at the sink finishing the dishes, and had pleaded with Tim, not just for her sake, but for Robby's.

"Tim, go to counseling for Robby. Do you really want to break up the only stability he's ever had? Please. You can go alone, or I'll go with you. We need professional help."

Getting up from the dinner table, Tim ignored Trish and started heading down to the basement. Throwing the dishtowel in the sink, Trish raced to the basement door and pushed the basement door closed.

"Tim, just listen to me for a minute," she began. When she knew she had Tim's attention, she sat down at the table.

"I need you to hear me this time. You say I don't understand you, but I don't think you even hear me when I talk. It's like you turn off as soon as I start saying anything you don't like. Do you even know how much I dread going to bed every night? Lying next to you, I feel your resentment. While you're downstairs in your office living in your pretend world, I'm upstairs lying in bed watching Lifetime TV and running out of red wine. I deserve more. I want to be your beauty queen again, and you won't let me."

Feeling emotionally spent, Trish pushed her hair away from her wet eyes and started cracking her knuckles out of nervousness. She laid her pounding head in her hands and braced for the yelling.

"I don't know what to tell you Trish. I'm forty and I need to make a difference before I die. You don't get me anymore. Rules! I feel like your rules are suffocating me, and no goddamn counseling is going to change that. My Facebook friends say my movie idea is good, but NOOOOOO, not you Trish."

Tim's face got a deeper red with each word he spat out.

"All you do is bitch about the money and the loan I want to take out. I'm sick and tired of your controlling bullshit. It's gotten worse. You've changed. You used to be more fun. I can't take it. You've got two choices. You can either deal with the fact that I make more money around here, and I'm going to start calling the shots, or you can run home to Mommy. What's it going to be? I'm done pussyfooting around."

Trish sat on the bench outside Shriver's, tears running down her cheeks as she remembered that night with its hateful words. That last screaming match was definitely the grand finale of "Trish and Tim." She couldn't handle any more pain. Trish was tired from this emotional roller coaster. She felt like a wrung-out dishtowel. She felt always blamed and never thanked.

If Tim thought that marriage counseling was pussyfooting around, then she guessed he was right. She had changed. Trish had grown up along the way, and she was tired of dragging him along kicking and screaming.

Trish still loved Tim, or maybe she was just confusing love with what they once shared. Either way, Tim's emotional chaos and his disconnection from everyday reality couldn't be ignored. The unhappier Tim became with himself, the angrier he became towards Trish. His occasional verbal abuse had escalated within the last three years of their marriage. Trish was sick of being his emotional punching bag.

If Tim wanted to get help and finally face his issues, then that was up to him. When she was 23, Trish thought it was her job to make Tim happy. Now, at 38, after several years of therapy, she knew that was up to him. Even though part of her wanted to stay – in hopes that Tim's demons would magically disappear – she knew it was time for her to save herself.

Leaving her eleven-year marriage was painful enough, but leaving Robby, that was more complicated. He was only two when she met Tim. Now, fifteen years later Trish truly felt like Robby was her own son. She wanted desperately to watch Robby grow up and have a family of his own, but she knew that the death of her marriage was also her cue to exit his life.

As a stepmom, her role was never easy, but now she confronted what felt like a permanent goodbye. There would be no visitation weekends, no "This year is your Christmas, next year is mine." In Trish's mind, leaving had never been an option before. Up until now, Robby was still a little boy speeding on that blue bumper car, who desperately needed her love and guidance.

———◦◦◦———

Now at seventeen, Robby would be all right. He still had a lot to learn, but with a reassuring goodbye hug, he had said calmly, "Don't cry Trish; it's kind of like you're Mary Poppins. You came and helped Dad and me…and now you have to go help another family. Don't worry, we're going to be fine, and you're going to be great."

The beginning of the end is always hard to talk about, but once remembered, it deserves to have its moment of destructive glory. In a marriage, there seems to be a series of precursory moments that lead up to the end. But if a woman reaches into the dark caverns of her heart's mind, she remembers there is usually one distinct moment; a moment when she's simply had enough, and the choice is made to leave; a moment that forever follows her in life's rear-view mirror.

As the New Jersey sun slowly moved across the powder blue sky, Trish felt a strange peace come over her. She knew now she was strong enough to choose herself. Starting over wouldn't be easy, but this time she was listening to her inner voice. Trish pressed her hands against the warm wood of Shriver's bench. She stood up, and slowly made her way through the crowd on the boardwalk.

Alone in My Sunshine Room

I sit in my room
In my sunshine room
And watch the light stream from the sky
Stream through the windows tall and high
Casting reflections that dazzle my eye

A window curtain plays its part
Its flowery pattern's a work of art
Upon the walls that were quite stark
Devoid of image, plain and dark

And unexpected spots appear
In nooks and corners far and near
Revealed realities once hidden
Now come to light, to my eye bidden

Then comes to mind new clarity of vision
Complexities dissolved into simple precision
With joy and blessings of life revealed
I embrace the day renewed and healed.

By Sharon Keys Gray

My Lost Art

I never thought a blank
piece of paper
could be my undoing.

It was so easy, in the beginning.
Me in my writing room
poems unbidden, bombarding the page.

Now, nothing!

I feel the swirling eddy
of self doubt rising
choking the words.

I pace.

Dust in the corner morphs
into a mountain of dirt
screaming to be cleaned.

I vacuum.

I open my "how to " books
but the suggested prompts
promptly immobilize me.

I check email; more due dates
for the anthology project.

Pinpricks of panic creep
up my neck, breathing
goes shallow.

I need chocolate!

Where are the urgent
phrases, clamoring
to be written?

Now, only brain static.

The words of my wall plaque mock:
"Here lives a poet"

By Harriet Singer

An Aging Rolling Stones Riff

'Twould be "Emotional Rescue"
if you could "Start Me Up"
since "Waiting on a Friend"
brings no "Satisfaction."
And we "Miss You" –
"Brown Sugar" and "Wild Horses."

Don't "Paint It Black"
dear "Ruby Tuesday."
I'm just a "Honky Tonk Woman"
who is "Slipping Away"
...who won't "Get Off My (her) Cloud"
...who can't "Tattoo You"
...who is told "She's So Cold."
NO!...once..."She Was Hot."

We've all learned "You Can't Always Get What You Want."
"Angie", my dear Angie - she knew that...
going on to have her "19th Nervous Breakdown."
She "Ain't Too Proud To Beg"
and she was no "Beast of Burden"
or "Back Street Girl."
She had no "Heart of Stone."
But oh, she cried, "What A Drag It Is Getting Old."

By Edda R. Pitassi

Brushed by a Stranger

Some nights I dream in feline
After a cat sitter's busy day
So many cats I've come to know
Lonely cats, happy cats
Calicos and tabbies, some large and some small
Cats on diets
Hungry cats weaving
Under the bed kitty…come see me please
Don't be afraid
Tuxedos at the window clustered
Waiting for their humans to return
Waiting to resume life as it should be
Intuitive cats who share their thoughts
In silence they speak to me
Cats on the sofa
Are they watching TV?
Do they dream in feline as I do?
Tasty treats, dry food that crunches
Where's my pate

Will I be brushed by a stranger today?

By Flo Shore

My Mother Never Told Me

My mother never told me

About the ancient mysteries,
Stories of the elders,
Secrets of the healers, and
How to remember.

She never told me

To listen to the ocean's music
Dance with the raindrops
Feel the power of moonlight and
Seek nature's wisdom.

My mother never told me

Risk is a necessary part of change
Change a necessary part of life, and
Fear is a natural by-product.

She never told me

About the deep well of loss
The longing of the soul
The dark caves of this spiritual journey
The divine light within.

And she never told me about
The peace found in silence
The solace found in prayer
The mystical in the mundane
The sacred in every day.

My mother never told me—
Her mother never told her.

By Harriet Singer

Some Day...Soon

I will speak fluent French
as I sit in a Paris café
and sip Pinot Noir
C'est bien

I will host a monthly discussion group
for my diverse friends willing
to suspend the superficial.

I will volunteer in the Sudan
and feed hungry-eyed dusty children
living in crumbling huts.

I will remain calm while talking
to the plumber, water
gushing from the toilet.

My poems will be published,
My house will be spotless.
My spider plants will thrive.

My hospice patient died Friday.
She was immobile except for her head.
That's the way with MS.
She was 57.

I find a seat in the second row
just as the bell rings.
Bonjour says the teacher.

By Harriet Singer

When Death Comes Late

When death comes late
   there are no friends to ease the way
   for they are long gone having made
   the journey sooner

When death come late
   the days are filled with vast emptiness
   and wonder at death's delay; could he
   have forgotten?

When death comes late
   the need for sustenance is subdued,
   made subservient to the desire to go;
   to be gone

When death comes late
   the smiling faces of the living pale
   even as memory finds the dead vibrant,
   alive, their laughter alluring

When death comes late
   the young are invisible ghosts whose
   antics heard of, never seen; refuse to
   appear to those awaiting death

When death comes late
   he is embraced with tears of joy
   and sighs of peace, come at last!

                              By Sharon Keys Gray

A Glance

It was a glance by merest chance
an unplanned aimless look askance
a turn of head and eyes, a dance
a movement to another stance

revealed a momentary site
of peace, of purity and light
the heavy flakes of white alight
on bark and branch and earth alike

and comforts all in quiet bliss
while I espy and ponder this
that but by chance I would have missed
this time, this taste of nature's kiss

By Sharon Keys Gray

Blessed by a Butterfly

By Flo Shore

It was late spring of 1964, and the end of a bitter winter. Summer was not far off. I could hardly wait for school to be out. Summer was synonymous with freedom – to roam the woods, go barefoot when Mom wasn't looking, and daydream in the shade of the big weeping willow tree in our backyard.

I enjoyed playing with the other children on my street. We played dodge ball, kickball, or climbed construction equipment that belonged to one of the neighbors who lived at the end of the street. We liked nothing more than to hop up into the well-worn black seats of the tractors, backhoes, and enormous front-end loaders and survey our universe of rust-colored dirt. Johnny, a self-appointed foreman, barked orders; there was work to be done!

Although I had fun, I sometimes preferred being all alone and would sneak away to read a book or sketch. I was a shy and pensive child, a dreamer with an unmistakably creative Piscean nature that lent itself to reflection.

One night that spring I decided not to play with the other children. It was a warm evening. I stood in the driveway with my dog, Fuzzy, watching the setting sun shine through the forsythia bushes, giving them a golden glow.

As I watched the sunlight slant across the forsythia, I saw a Monarch butterfly flutter around the side of the house and across the gravel driveway. I stood still. Its vibrant orange and black colors caught my eye. For once, I wasn't thinking about my unfinished math homework that left me stumped, or the seemingly endless array of chores my mother glibly dispensed, or even the cliquish girls at school.

The butterfly, this marvel of nature, came to light on my upper arm. Riveted, I instinctively knew not to move or even breathe for fear that it would startle and fly off. It felt like several minutes had elapsed as it rested there, though in fact it had been mere seconds.

Although the butterfly's resting on my arm seemed like a miracle to me, I did not mention it the next day at school. I didn't really trust anyone to understand and was certain they would laugh at me. A scornful "so what?" or "who cares!" would be the likely responses from my fourth grade classmates.

That evening however, I needed to find the magic again. My plan was to stand in just the same spot at around the same time and see what might happen. I stood still and silent in the driveway. Again, the butterfly flitted by me. Would it remember me and alight? I held my breath and waited. To my amazement the butterfly rested on my outstretched arm. I examined its delicate, fragile feelers—fine and brown. Was it examining me as well? Perhaps it recognized me by my short pixie haircut, fair skin, and hazel eyes?

On the third night, I waited again in the driveway at the same time in the evening for what seemed an eternity. The sun was beginning to set, and I was afraid I might soon hear my mother's lilting voice calling me in for the night. I felt a strange tickle as something touched my left ear. My involuntary response was to brush whatever it was away quickly. I felt sick to my stomach and my heart sank. Had I wounded my dear friend in haste? I looked down, and to my relief I had only brushed away a leaf that had drifted down from one of the tall maple trees.

Grateful to have caused no harm, I continued my vigil. Sure enough my companion returned. The Monarch paused tentatively for just a moment on my arm. At that moment I felt deeply attuned to nature. I had often wondered, what would it be like to converse with all of the animals, birds, and even insects? What incredible stories they might tell! Now I seemed to have been given the opportunity to know this one beautiful creature and to appreciate how fleeting its life was destined to be.

By the fourth night, it had become a comforting ritual to step onto the gravel driveway and wait for a sign. The stillness was once again a welcome change from schoolwork, chores, and even kickball or climbing on the construction equipment. The sun sparkled, and the forsythia looked like pure gold. This time, however, I wasn't so lucky. This time there was no butterfly.

Although disappointed, I wasn't at all surprised. Everyone knows butterflies don't last forever. For a few days I felt special to have gained the trust of so magical a creature.

The evening shadows widened as I went inside. The screen door banged behind me. I left my dreamy world of insect friends and the wonders of nature somewhere out there. I consciously decided to commit to memory the events of the previous three nights. It surely was not my imagination, and I would not allow anyone to tell me otherwise.

I keep hoping to this day that another such friend might take a shine to me. And to this day, I always stop and stand perfectly still whenever butterflies are near.

Childhood

Cheers and Beers! To Grandpop Joe

By Maureen Barry

Row houses line neighborhood streets. Steps lead to porches where American flags and pots of geraniums bring color to an otherwise concrete and gray tableau.

Everyone in the neighborhood knows that I am Joe and Mary's granddaughter. "Hello, Maureen!" they shout as they sit on their front porch gliders. I always give them a wave or a hello. Vinnie Billotti, a boy a couple years older than I, lives three houses down from my grandparents. He usually yells an obnoxious comment like, "Hey, you're looking good, girl."

Like I care what he thinks!

It is here at 63rd and Greenway Avenue in Philadelphia that Grandpop Joe Garvey teaches me the fine art of pouring beer when I am 10 years old. Grandpop walks to the refrigerator and grabs the quart of Ortlieb's beer, along with American cheese and ham. Then he goes to the cabinet where he takes two juice glasses off the shelf, along with crackers and peanut butter for snacks. Next, he takes his seat at the head of the table. I take my seat next to him.

He picks up the quart of beer. "Maureen, there is a special trick to pouring a glass of beer. Pour it so it forms a one-inch white foamy head."

Grandpop Joe pours the beer so it slides down the inside of the juice glass. As the beer fills the glass, a perfect one-inch foamy white head forms.

"Now always make sure it doesn't overflow. You don't want to waste any of that good beer," he stresses. Then he slides the quart of beer to me.

"Your turn," he grins.

Grandpop looks like Clark Gable — dashing and rakish with jet-black hair and a grin the ladies die for. He is so handsome my grandmother worries she may lose him. But I know better.

He calls her "my Mary." They have been married going on forty-three years and have two children. One is my mother, Betty Garvey O'Rourke.

I admit I am nervous. I hold my glass in my left hand. I grasp the bottle of beer firmly in my right. I carefully glide the beer down the inside of the glass. A white, foamy head forms. I can't see my grin, but I feel it spreading from ear to ear. After the beer settles, we toast each other's success with a clink of our glasses. I take a big gulp of my beer.

"Slow down," Grandpop warns with a laugh. "You know you only get one glass, Maureen. I don't want your mother getting mad at me for giving you a little beer."

"Ahhhhh, there's nothing like a cold beer," I smile, imitating him.

"The evidence is on your upper lip. You have a white moustache," he laughs.

I slide my tongue across my upper lip wiping away my foamy moustache. I am proud of my accomplishment. Not everyone knows how to pour the perfect glass of beer. But now I do!

Like most ten-year-olds, I am at that awkward stage. I am skinny, still growing. I wonder what might pop out on my chest. I have thick, long brown hair that my grandmother loves to make into finger curls. Rolling a strand of wet hair with a piece of cloth secured by bobby pins makes the perfect finger curl. I sit patiently as my grandmother gives me her undivided attention. If my head isn't bouncing with curls, my hair is pulled back and swinging a ponytail.

But it is those times with Grandpop that I feel most special, most pretty.

———◦———

I also like playing alone in my make-believe world. When he hears me talking to my imaginary friends, Grandpop is as amused as I am.

"Hey Maureen, who's in there with you? When are we going to meet your special friends?" Grandpop asks in a teasing tone, as he walks down the hallway past my bedroom door.

"Oh, if only you knew, Grandpop. There are a lot of people in here," I laugh.

I am my own best friend, along with my dolls and my Flintstone and Jetson collections. These collections are toys modeled after cartoon shows on television. The Flintstones take me to the caveman age; the Jetsons fly me to the space age. My imaginary worlds entertain me for hours. I also spend time reading my Nancy Drew mystery books.

———◦———

It is here in my grandparents' house, away from the squabbling of my brothers and sisters back home, that I find my own little sanctuary.

I love my grandparents' kitchen with its yellow and chrome Formica table. Pot roast on a Sunday afternoon fills my senses. Anticipating the taste of creamy mashed potatoes with lots of melted butter, salt, and pepper makes my mouth water. This kitchen is where I have my first cooking lessons.

"Grandmom, how do I make mashed potatoes?"

"Maureen, get the potato peeler and peel the skin from the potatoes. Then, slice the potato in half and cut each half into four. Put the potatoes into a pot of water, add some chopped onion and salt, then boil the potatoes until they are soft."

While the potatoes cook, I set the table using my grandmother's fancy crocheted tablecloth. For Sunday dinners the white china with intricate pink flowers comes out. I set a place for each family member: a plate, fork, knife, spoon, and a napkin. My Uncle Jim, my mother's brother, and his family always join us. Grandmom's brother, Uncle Bill, and his wife, Aunt Mae, visit, too. The table settings offer a formal elegance, but our gathering is anything but formal. Everyone talks and laughs. After setting the table, I return to the kitchen to do more food preparation, cutting string beans and learning how to boil them gently. I am Grandmom's sous chef and I love being her helper!

———————

As a 10-year-old visiting my grandparents, I was lucky to know my great-grandmother, Elizabeth McVeigh. She went blind in old age and lived with my grandparents. She sat in her armchair in the living room. I don't know if she heard the floor creak or her hearing was super sensitive, but she'd ask, "Who's there?" whenever I entered the room.

Watching her, I learned about blind people and how they compensate for their loss of vision.

"Come here, Maureen," she would say. "Rest your head on my lap."

I loved taking my afternoon naps on her lap. She ran her fingers through my hair, and her loving touch soothed me to sleep.

My grandfather worked as a fireman for the City of Philadelphia. I remember one time he told me how he had found a man burned to death. He described the helplessness of the situation, "Maureen, there just wasn't anything left to the body." His sad tone revealed his compassion for how tragic life can be.

Many days during that summer of 1960, Grandpop took me fishing and crabbing along the New Jersey Shore. There was always lots of activity on the dock as well as on the water. People lounged in beach chairs as they munched on sandwiches and watched their lines bob up and down

"Maureen, good cast!" shouts Grandpop.

I seldom snag the line. I practice casting the line, waiting patiently, and then reeling the line in slow and steady. But, nothing!

"Cast the line again, Maureen," Grandpop coaches.

Time passes slowly, sometimes too slowly for a ten-year-old. I do a lot of sitting. The water glistens from sparkles created by the bright sunshine. Waves bounce against the pilings from the motion of motorboats cutting through the water. The sound of motors grinding their gears together fills the hot summer air.

Grandpop shares snacks of pretzels and peanuts as I wait for my fish to bite. Sometimes I feel a tug. I reel in my line only to find my bait gone.

"Ah..." I sigh with disappointment.

"It takes time, Maureen," Grandpop nods. "Don't give up."

Grandpop's unending patience guides me in baiting my hook.

"Be careful, don't snag your finger on the hook," he warns.

I bait the hook and cast the line far out. My reel spins, there's a strong tugging and I reel in my line.

"Grandpop, Grandpop, I got one!" I shout as the line bends.

"Take your time; you don't want to lose it," he says.

At the end of the line is a huge flopping flounder. I jump up and down with excitement.

———◦———

Saturdays at my grandparent's house are for cleaning. I know how to clean because I do household chores at home. So when Grandmom asks me to help her, I willingly volunteer. As I finish cleaning the kitchen's white porcelain sink one morning, the back door opens and Grandpop enters carrying a brown paper bag. He wears his fedora hat and brown corduroy jacket. In the brown bag – a quart of Ortlieb's.

"This beer should be real cold by noon so we can have it with our lunch," Grandpop chuckles as he puts his beer in the refrigerator. "You'll need a break by then. You've been working hard."

Time moves in slow motion, and very little is said between us. I set the table for lunch: plates, utensils and paper napkins. I watch and smile as he hangs his jacket on the cellar door hook and places his hat on the shelf. He seldom changes his daily routine. This is something I observe on my weekend visits.

Every other morning he walks to the Greenway Tavern at Greenway and Woodland Avenues to buy his beer and run errands.

Known as "the Avenue," this is where clothing shops and hardware stores line the street.

This is where my grandpop runs errands and socializes with neighbors who meander along Woodland Avenue. Sometimes I go with him.

"Hi Maureen. I can't believe how grown up you are. Joe, how's Mary? Everybody okay?" asks Lou, his neighbor.

"We're okay. Everybody's healthy. No complaints," responds Grandpop.

"Did you watch the Friday Night Fights?" asks Lou.

"I always watch the fights, and Joe Louis gave Rocky a good run for his money," Grandpop says. "Gotta run, Lou."

Grandpop takes my hand. "Take care," Grandpop nods, as we walk off.

———◦◦◦———

As I said, Grandpop looked a lot like Clark Gable. Women's heads turned whenever he walked into a room, and Grandmom was possessive of him. One day that summer, she grabbed me by the hand.

"Come on, Maureen, we're going for a walk," she announces with an edge in her tone.

I know we were going to the Greenway Tavern. I guess she thinks Grandpop is taking too long getting his beer. I suspect she imagines him flirting with another woman. She doesn't walk that day; she charges down the street in a frenzied rush.

We enter the dimly lit tavern where the sign reads "Ladies Entrance." Back then the corner bar was never the gathering place for women. Women were expected to enter by a side door and sit quietly in the dining area.

Grandmom and I sit in a big brown wooden booth. It's not time for lunch, so I order a root beer and peanuts. Grandpop immediately joins us. No signs of flirtatious women to be found; nevertheless, my grandmother has made her point just by showing up. I can almost hear her announce to the room, "Joe Garvey belongs to me. He is my husband!" No one hears her because we are the only ones there.

Grandpop always excused her behavior, I think because he loved her unconditionally. Their opposing temperaments created a balance that lasted for fifty-seven years of marriage.

———◦◦◦———

I was twenty-four when Grandpop died. Our entire family was vacationing together at the New Jersey Shore. When he finally asked my dad to drive him to the hospital, his prostate cancer had spread. He was dying. The family stayed with him around the clock to make sure he was comfortable. He lay moaning, and his skin turned yellowish. It was pure anguish for me to watch him suffer. He had helped me all my life, yet I was powerless now to help him. After a little over a week, he succumbed to the disease. He was seventy-four.

His body was transported to Philadelphia where he had an Irish wake, a farewell as well as a celebration, with many firefighters in attendance. His body was laid to rest in a coffin in his living room at 63rd and Greenway Avenue.

I was in shock, in denial, and very angry that this man who meant so much to me was gone. After everyone left on the night of his wake, I stayed at the house with Grandmom. I didn't want her to be by herself.

After she went to bed, I sat on the stairs staring at Grandpop in his casket. The undertaker had covered his face with a powdery cake make-up. It didn't look like my Grandpop, my Clark Gable. As I sat staring at him, tears rolled down my face. I'm not sure how long I sat there, but I sobbed until I was exhausted. Finally I went to bed. The next day we buried him under a big shade tree at Holy Cross Cemetery in Lansdowne, a small town just west of Philadelphia.

Years have passed since Joe Garvey's death, but he drifts in and out of my memory, much like the warm July breezes of that summer when he taught me so many of life's lessons. Now, whenever I pour myself a beer, I return in my mind's eye to the kitchen at 63rd and Greenway Avenue. I see sunlight streaming through the window onto the Formica table. I hear my Grandpop say, "You have a white moustache, Maureen."

I hear the clink of our glasses as we toast ourselves and all that life has to offer.

A Portrait of Four Friendships

By Vicki McKeefery

As I organize photographs from my digital camera into folders on my laptop, I pause at the picture of the four of us smiling with our glasses raised in a birthday toast.

"The girls," I murmur softly.

The camera caught one tall, honey-haired woman with glasses and a wide, easy grin; an athletic-looking brunette, deeply tanned with a steady gaze; a blonde with an impish smile, and me, with a cap of cropped brown hair and a bright smile.

These women are not my relatives, but we've gone through our whole lives together. We're not young anymore. We've got wrinkles and gray hair. We're heavier than we once were. Yet as I look into these familiar faces upraised for the camera, I see, clearly, the girls that we were.

Beckett was the math teacher on my teaching team, and I met her the first year I taught junior high school history. She told me that when she was in college, she was dubbed Beckett, which was her last name. The moniker stuck. Five months passed before I discovered her first name was Linda and by then Beckett just seemed to fit. My initial impression of Beckett was that she looked too young to be a teacher. With her honey-colored pony tail, round owlish glasses, and a wide, slow smile, she seemed more like a junior high school girl, except she was much taller than most of our students.

Beckett kept her toothbrush in the faculty room and brushed her teeth after lunch. She only drank water, never soda, but she loved martinis. When the rest of us were teaching in Villager skirts and high heels, Beckett wore slacks and flats. Beckett had a long-time boyfriend from college, so we never saw her on the weekends.

Calm and steady, Beckett's independent outlook and good sense helped me gain confidence through that first challenging year of teaching.

We met in the faculty room during our free periods. Under fluorescent lights that glared and buzzed, we sat on thrift shop sofas. I confided my problems to Beckett, since as members of the same team, we taught the same ninth grade students, just different subjects. In this tiny office space Beckett conducted my therapy sessions.

"I'm teaching kids my little sister's age," I moaned, slumping on the sofa. "I don't even feel that much older."

Beckett laughed in an easy, relaxed manner, and tucked a wayward strand of hair behind her ear. "Our students don't know how old you are. Remember, to them, you seem like a grown-up. They probably think you're forty."

I shuddered at the thought.

I remember the day that I walked down the hall, ears ringing from my noisy classroom, and noticed that Sam Ramsay's door was open.

Sam taught history on the other ninth grade team. All the students' eyes were focused on him; he seemed like a magician to me. Students sat transfixed. They obediently bent to write his words in their notebooks.

Deflated, I shuffled into the faculty room for more "therapy."

"Beckett," I wailed, sitting next to her on the lumpy sofa, "my students don't behave even remotely like those in Sam Ramsay's class. You can hear a pin drop in there. They actually listen to every word he says."

She pushed her glasses up the bridge of her nose, and then leaned in toward me, elbows to knees. "Someone shot spitballs at the board this afternoon during my seventh period class. It's bad enough that I have no clue who did it, but now my board is gross too."

Her eyes rolled so comically I couldn't help but laugh.

"I know we'll get better," she continued seriously. "We'll know what to watch out for next time, and our discipline will improve, so we'll be more effective. We just have to hang in there and not give up."

Her sense of humor and advice buoyed my spirits. I felt better. Beckett always made me feel better.

———◦◉◦———

Drea arrived my second year of teaching. With her chestnut brown hair bristling with pencils and her organized, confident air, she was the epitome of a math teacher. Drea, short for Andrea, was logical . . . a planner. She created an outline for a whole semester, not just a week or two at a time. Using the outline, she calculated how many chapters she needed to teach each semester in order to finish the book, and, of course, her classes always finished the book. Drea graded papers in her free periods instead of chatting in the faculty room, so she had time to coach the cheerleaders after school and chaperone their games at night.

She favored salty snacks and beer. She could play bridge, ski and scuba dive, all with skill. After her first year, we became roommates. I learned that Drea saw life through the lens of mathematical order: All problems have solutions, the universe operates logically, and fairness always counts. She felt if you applied those parameters to clear up problems, then you were free to savor life's opportunities.

Drea showed me that I could give my life direction and control instead of constantly reacting to what life handed out. She kept me grounded.

One Friday night in our apartment, as we hashed over some injustice that occurred earlier at school, I pulled chicken out of the oven in our galley kitchen. The open oven door, plus my rear, which was jammed against the cabinets behind me, blocked Drea's path to the small dining space beyond. She slapped down her fistful of utensils on the one small counter by the cabinets and fixed me with an intense brown-eyed gaze. I knew the next remarks would have no preamble, but would cut to the heart of her thoughts.

"We simply have to get out of this apartment. We don't know anyone here in this complex. We need to meet some new people who don't talk about school. We have to get out and meet some guys."

"Let's give the singles bars a try," Drea continued. "We can make a list of all the singles clubs within a fifteen-mile radius. Every Friday night we can try a different one."

I really hated bars. "It's a meat market in those places. I don't like the idea of being on display and hunting for guys. It's like shopping for people. It's noisy and I hate beer. Things should happen more naturally; it's too contrived. You know that I think we have a better chance to meet guys at universities when we get our masters degrees."

Drea nailed me with the determined stare again. "Right now, this minute, no guys are going to fall through the roof and land here on our doorstep, so let's get out there. We haven't even enrolled in graduate school yet. We could die waiting for things to 'happen naturally.' Or we could always just date guys at school."

She knew that would get me. "Never date people at work" was a motto for both of us. So, out we went. And she was right. Just getting out of the apartment and meeting new people did make me feel better than sitting at home watching "That Girl" on TV have all the fun.

Of course, she was there when I met my husband . . . where else? In a bar. But I was there when she met hers at graduate school. This irony had a certain mathematical symmetry.

———◦———

Celia came to our school to teach English two years after Drea. Slight, with short blonde hair, she sparkled like a firecracker and talked with rapid-fire delivery. The air around her seemed to crackle with electricity like an energy field. Since she wasn't in the history department, did not teach ninth grade, and was five years younger than I, Celia and I might not have become friends except for two developments.

We both drove colorful VW bugs. Hers was baby blue and mine was neon orange. We loved those cars, and we loved swapping stories about road trips we took in them. We even loved griping about how the heaters never worked right and the rounded trunks held almost nothing!

Second, Celia loved to go to the nightclubs and bars. She enthusiastically embraced Drea's social plan to meet men, and her enthusiasm infused a new spirit into our Friday night singles ritual.

Celia liked sipping on Black Russians and devouring chocolate candy. She joined the ski club with Drea and the theater group at school. She organized parties at her house and recommend after-school events. *Animated, energetic* and *tireless* are words that best describe Celia.

Celia was also a worrier, and so was I. We found satisfaction in imagining "what if" scenarios for crises; this while Beckett had already adjusted to the situation, and Drea had made a decision how to fix it.

Celia was my advice columnist, my "Dear Abby." Unlike the rest of us, she rented an apartment close to school, which became an easy place to gather after work. Her homey, one-bedroom apartment with the gabled windows became the scene of after-school get-togethers and heart-to-heart talks. Many times I climbed the winding back stairway of that old two-story home, which deposited guests directly on Celia's kitchen threshold. One day, after a long afternoon faculty meeting, I decided to stop at her house on my way home. I knocked on her kitchen door.

As the door opened, Celia's energy seemed to shimmer around her.

"Come in! Come in!" she said, grabbing my arm and pulling me the rest of the way into the kitchen. "Sit down over here on this stool while I finish. I'm cooking meatza pie and I'm just ready to pop it in the oven. Do you want something to drink? Let's have tea. I'll put the water on. Want some chocolate chip cookies? Or how about some Hershey Kisses? What about that faculty meeting? Some bombshell he dropped, huh?"

She laughed and waved a wooden spoon as she talked, pulling open cupboards, and filling up casserole dishes while she worked. All I could do was sit and listen. I knew I wouldn't get a word in edgewise.

Drawing me into one of her overstuffed chairs in the living room and handing me a cup of tea, she plopped into the other chair as she asked about my latest heartthrob.

"I don't know if I want to keep dating Tom," was a statement that would elicit an hour's worth of questions and analysis.

Celia was a good listener. I could tell when she was really absorbed in my story because she nervously twisted her fingers. Talking out a problem with Celia always made the problem seem smaller and helped me feel better. She remembered important bits of conversation too, especially dates. Weeks after a conversation, she would recall the correct day to ask how some special event turned out.

As the years wore on, Celia became disillusioned with teaching.

"How much English grammar can you instruct over and over again? I honestly can't listen to the snickers of eighth grade boys as I teach the verbs lay and lie one more time without going nuts," she joked, sometimes without a trace of humor.

Later it was, "Discipline is driving me nuts. I wish I were taller and weighed more. It's hard to be an authority figure when the kids are taller than you."

Finally, after six years, she gave up teaching and became an editor of medical journals.

The four of us never worked together again.

———◦———

Forty years later, I know what happens after Celia leaves our school. Celia met her husband at her new job. She has two boys who are in graduate school. She spends countless hours traveling to her hometown to care for ill parents and a disabled brother, for whom she is the sole relative. She has no plans to retire. "I think I'll have to work until I'm eighty!" she told me.

And as for the others? After dating the college boyfriend for eleven years, Beckett marries him. They move to an old farmhouse and have three sons. She teaches math for another thirty-five years before retiring.

Drea marries the guy she met at school the same summer I marry the guy I met in the bar. Drea raises five children, some his, some theirs. When her husband has heart surgery at forty-five and later, when he loses his job, she keeps the whole blended family on course. Drea teaches math for thirty-four years, mostly in a different district than the one where we met. She retired right after Beckett.

Me? I'm still married, and my husband and I have two children, a son and a daughter.

Over the years, Celia is the one who helps keep the four of us in touch. She sends e-mail reminders to "the girls" about our quarterly birthday dinners, which we started soon after we all married and began to lose touch. We depended on those birthday dinners, and the lines of communication that the dinners nurtured.

In the beginning when we first met and worked together, we supported each other for specific reasons: to help each other cope with work problems, or to provide a social group to meet other people. We worked together and lived near each other, so we didn't have to try hard to get together.

After we married, when our children were little, and then again when we all went back to work at different places, long stretches of time passed when we didn't have a lot of contact. We easily could have drifted apart. But, we were lucky. Nobody was transferred out of the area, and each of us gave our scheduled dinners priority. Those four annual meetings became sacred. In between, we called each other for advice, encouragement, and fun. We managed to keep up with enough events, both large and small, that our friendship gradually became a treasured support in our lives. Then, as additional years added their weight, we woke up to the uniqueness of our relationship. We began to realize and appreciate the length of our friendship and its shared history.

A few weeks ago, we had our latest dinner gathering. This dinner is our late summer one: August, my birthday.

I am newly retired and nervous about all my new unstructured time. "What do you guys do to keep busy, so you don't go crazy in retirement? Should I tutor? Or maybe teach a night class?" I anxiously ask.

Beckett leans back in the restaurant booth and answers first. She laughs that easy laugh of hers and tucks back that strand of hair. "Go easy on yourself. You'll find plenty to do. Until then, enjoy the free time." Then she rolls her eyes.

Drea fixes me with her steady gaze, sets down her beer, and nods her head in agreement. "You will figure this out. In time you will devise a plan."

Celia looks disgusted, throws out her arms to encompass us all and raps out, "Shut up about all your free time you three. I may wither away right in my cubicle."

I laugh, and they do too.

Beckett says she wants to stay in her farmhouse forever. Drea is certain she will move to a retirement center. Celia is not ready to think about selling her house yet. I am uncertain what I will do, so I worry about it.

I wonder out loud, "When is the right age to sell your house? If you move to a retirement center, do you stay around your friends or move to be closer to your children? What do you do when your children don't live anywhere near each other? Do you choose between them?"

Drea butters her roll, but she stops and looks at me with her intent gaze. "There's a logical solution; you just haven't thought it up yet."

Beckett sips her martini and agrees. "Be patient. You have some years before you have to make decisions like that."

I look over and see that Celia is twisting her fingers in her lap as I talk. She seizes the moment and toasts us all with her Black Russian.

"Take my advice and don't think about selling yet if the answer's not clear. Besides, none of you is allowed to move too far away. That's an order. So here's to us. Raise your glasses high! May we have many more birthday gatherings so we can figure out the answers to these questions and more!"

I chuckle at us all. Some things never change.

That was two weeks ago. Lately, as I ponder life and change, I wonder what the future holds for us. I know how lucky I am to enjoy them. These women know things about me that my parents and my siblings do not. They have experienced things with me that neither my children nor my husband has.

So, I take a moment to really look at that photograph taken on my sixty-fifth birthday: four people, each one an individual in her own right. Each one shaped my life for the better. Forty years of friendship, four mature women; but to me, we'll always be "the girls."

Relationships

Josie: The Answer to a Prayer You Don't Know How to Pray

By Jodi Monster

Lobster salad must be served chilled, cradled between buttery halves of a lightly toasted white roll. Chowder must be served piping hot, in a mug, with hard crackers on the side. It is not necessary to provide both; one, when offered at noontime with a strong, cold beer, will do the trick. I went with the lobster roll on the day I ordered Jim off his duff.

Jim is my son, who was raised by the sea in the cottage where I still live. There is a small stretch of caramel-colored beach just across the road, and a moored raft for sunning. There are rocky out crops for jumping, and mud flats for clamming—he had, in other words, a picture postcard life. A life entirely of a piece with his marrying the girl next door, of whom I have always been terribly fond. Louise is her name, and they have given me grandchildren. Three, all grown. Which gives me pause, to think I have lived here that long–some fifty odd years. So long that I catch myself some days taking it for granted—the sea and the sky and the great Norway maple that shelters us all; so long that I catch myself forgetting, sometimes, how odd it is that through my wide kitchen window, which faces off to the east, I have observed five decades' worth of the most intimate goings-on in Betty's life.

Betty is Louise's mother, and it was after she was picked up by the police that I invited Jim to lunch. A patrolman plodding towards home along the busy coastal road, just at its most treacherous turn, spotted Betty. Her wanderings were something of a given, Betty's, within the secluded confines of our cove—just one more piece of local color. The neighbors watched for her, and waved to her, and set their kitchen clocks by her twice-daily constitutional along the quiet beach road. By heart they knew her unruly crop of white hair and the steep, forward slope of her shoulders; by heart they knew her outfit, which never varied. On the day Betty was brought home in the squad car, she was wearing checkered polyester golf pants with a coordinating, collared shirt, over which she had miss-buttoned a scratchy wool cardigan, one of the many she had knit for herself in the bleak years after her first husband died.

Truth to tell, Betty never paid me much mind. It stung at first, I'll admit, the way she kept to herself, and I wondered if had we made a mistake. My husband and I were second wave, you see, those who came to the cove after it had been formed up—which really shouldn't have mattered, except that there were certain circles wherein it did.

Betty and her husband Donald were first wave. Their proud and sturdy cohort laid a road where there was none, and divvied an unused coastal parcel into small lots. And for their trouble, they were called clam diggers by those with the good sense to live up town. That was 1938 or thereabouts—a time of gathering compassion and courage. And when that day finally came, when the righteous rose up against the mean — oh, how Donald wished to serve. To do his duty, as he saw it. But Donald was an accountant who just happened to work for a munitions concern. This was his service, the draft board said, and they deferred him to it. And I will never forget the look on his face the night he told Betty that his last appeal had been denied, and that he would stay home while others went off to fight. There are those who believe his girls bore the full brunt of his anger and shame, and there are those who say he took it out upon himself. And then there are those, like me, who believe that he did both—and I had, after all, a front row seat.

For years I watched as he worked furiously, and was promoted. I noticed when he joined the Rotary, and tried his hand at painting and pinochle. And I knew when, on doctor's orders, he and Betty both took up golf: "Nothing like a little fresh air and exercise." And then one day when their girls were grown, on the eve of a big nor'easter, Donald went out as always to pull the girls' rowboat. The boat washed ashore over to Indian Neck, but his body was never found.

Betty grieved sincerely and at length. For years I watched from my window as she sat of evening with nothing but a small sandwich and a large highball on the TV tray before her. We were so close in those moments I might have reached out across the privet hedge that divided her narrow lot from my narrower one; we were so close in those moments I might have averted my eyes. And it is mine, now, to confess that I did neither.

We co-existed in this way for many years, until the day that Betty ran into Harold at a Historical Society tea and her life began anew. Harold took her to dinner and booked cruises; he bought her a car, which came to a bad end, and in startling short order he had sold his big house uptown and moved into her small one by the shore. And then one night about three years back, after a fried clam supper, Harold too was called home, ushered peacefully to his rest with a full belly and a few stray batter crumbs about his lips.

I rejoiced for Betty during the happy years of her second marriage, although she never knew it. We'd wave our hellos in passing and that was all, a state of neighborly affairs I had long since stopped taking personally because I had long since come to understand: Betty was simply too obedient for generosity. For over the years, Louise, who spent as much time at my house as she did at her own, had revealed much more than she knew. There were the facts, of course: that Betty's father was a minister, and quite an unforgiving one at that. And then there were the gleanings: that the God of Betty's father favored but a few. It was a brutal chain of command—father, then God—and Betty served it with all of her might, even to the exclusion, or so it seemed to me, of her girls.

Louise did not say as much, of course. She was not disloyal, just glad of a place where she could share her musings. It was I who brought the circle 'round, in my own mind at least, when I saw Betty teetering on high ladders to scrape the salt from her windows and steaming her sheets flat in August when the rest of us simply hung ours out to air in the breeze. It was I who couldn't help but conclude that by these measures Betty declared the article of her faith: that the four corners of her small property marked the exact boundaries of her responsibility. And I lamented.

———※———

In the aftermath of Harold's death, many things became clear. The telephone bill had not been paid, Louise discovered, after days of not being able to reach her mom. The milk had gone sour and the lettuce to rot, Louise found, one day when she arrived with a few sweets for Betty's freezer. And there was an altercation with a mailbox a few streets over, Louise learned, when a reluctant neighbor called to ask when she might be able to remove her mother's car from his front lawn. It was at this point that Louise took her mother's keys, and arranged for the bus that would take Betty out grocery shopping and over to the Silver Sneakers exercise class at the Y several times each week. But Betty refused to go.

There came a string of caretakers then, all of whom Betty chased away. She accused them of stealing, and made sport out of spilling her food. She threw shoes at the girls and insulted them; she called the police. Always when the officers arrived, she asked them please, pretty-please to take her to Grandma Alice's house.

One after another the girls left in tears, until finally the agency refused to send any more and Betty was left with only Louise to provide for her — which she did rather perfunctorily, in my poor view. And so had it came to pass that Betty was found at dusk walking along the coastal highway all alone: cocktail time had rolled around, and when Betty discovered that her cupboard had run dry, she had simply decided to walk to the package store all the way over in Stony Creek. When the policeman pulled up beside her, he found that she was folded nearly in half around a gallon jug of the white zinfandel she loved, which she was clutching to her bosom as if for dear life.

Josie came as a last resort, on a day to be cherished. She came in a late model Saab, driven by people Louise did not know. I was just washing the grinds from my coffee pot when they arrived, and I watched them step from the car and take in the day. The water in front of Betty's house ran cobalt, with navy underneath. A cormorant fished out by cow and calf, a pair of granite boulders abandoned to the seabed by the glacier when it fled. Closer to shore, fat gulls roosted on the boat poles and dinghies bobbed on sure lines. In between, out by where the bigger boats were moored, a school of snapper blues had stalled in its run. The fish breached by turns; several at a time they jumped high into the summer sun that refracted off their scales, and Betty, I could see, was in the basement, vacuuming cobwebs from the low beams.

Louise came out onto the front walk to greet them. How, I imagine she must have asked, will this work, since she has sent all the others away? And then Josie turned away from the water so that I could see her face, and my coffee grinds splattered to the floor.

———— ◦ ————

On the day she arrived, Louise sped Josie in through the backdoor and up the stairs to her room. In the room there was a scuffed pine dresser topped with an old TV, and a drying rack hung with two sets of thin towels. In the closet there were six sets of light blue surgical scrubs, one for each of Josie's workdays. Louise had purchased these in advance of Josie's coming, she explained, in hope that Betty might better accept an aide in uniform. Josie's fingers found a medallion that hung loose around her neck, and rested there.

"You no worry, Ma'am Louise. I take your mother good care."

"Who are you?" Betty hissed when Josie arrived on the front porch, dressed in her work clothes and ready to begin.

The front porch offered a panoramic view of the cove, and in the second year of their marriage, Harold had arranged for it to be enclosed and winterized. An anniversary present for them both, he had called it, and insisted that they take their meals there from that point forward. Betty had vehemently resisted this change, and then warmed to it such that she continued, after his passing, to sit down to breakfast and lunch there daily, although without him she ate poorly.

Terribly! For weeks I watched her subsist on whole wheat toast from a freezer-burned loaf, cottage cheese, and peanut butter crackers—until I began to arrive at lunchtime with heaping plates of food I pretended were leftovers that I implored her to help me eat.

"My, but aren't you cunning," Betty said, taking the food from my hands. And then she sent me on my way.

"Ma'am Betty, I am Josie. I come to take you care," Josie said.

"What's wrong with your face?" Betty demanded.

Louise, who had secreted herself in the kitchen to monitor Josie's settling, rushed to intercede. "Mother, this is Josie," she said. "I came by yesterday to tell you about her—surely you remember? She is very nice, and she has come to help you."

"Get rid of her," Betty hissed.

"Now, mother," Louise tried to reason, but Betty pushed back her chair and rose to her feet.

"I rather think I'd know if I needed any help," Betty said on her way into the kitchen to fix a cup of Sanka with lukewarm water from the tap.

———◦◦◦———

Josie's room had a picture window, and a view over the beach. It was August and the days were warm, and unspeakably long, but in the evenings, she fastened the window tight. She had been raised to fear snakes and spiders and most especially a draft, but no one, it seemed, had thought to warn her about the spirits that rose on the endless plainsong of the tide.

She pulled a faded towel from the rack. At night there was amnesia, and rest, but every morning the startle was the same, to be reckoned with as one reckons with the sun. She drew water into the basin and leaned in towards the mirror, supplicant before the day. And then she washed and went downstairs.

Betty was already up, although she had not dressed. She sat in an old nylon nightdress and gazed out upon the morning. There had been a recent storm, and the tide line was drawn in the malodorous, black seaweed it had loosed from the rocks, now dead and full of flies. Of late the cove had hired professionals to rake the spoiled seaweed away, at which Betty sniffed in disdain. In her day, you cared for your frontage and you did not complain.

"I bring you breakfast, Ma'am Betty," Josie said, coming onto the porch.

Betty spun around. "Leave me alone!" she shouted.

"Ma'am Betty, I bring you breakfast." Josie said. And then she set down her pretty, plastic tray where Betty could see it. "See, I bring you French toast and orange juice. I bring you coffee and some warm milk." Also on the tray was one perfect pink rose from the rugosa bushes that grew along the sea wall, in a bud vase Josie had ransacked an old sideboard to find.

"Go away!" Betty shouted, but Josie did not flinch. Rather, she began to transfer the contents of her tray onto a placemat; Betty watched her, as if the meal might be tempting after all, and then she reached for the vase. "This belongs in Grandma Alice's room!" she cried.

"Ma'am Betty, I am Josie. I come to take you care...," Josie started to say, but then she stopped because Betty bent suddenly forward towards the floor, as if there were something she had dropped.

She fished around the floor for a minute, and when she sat back up, Betty held in her hand one filthy terrycloth slipper. She sat still for a minute, and Josie thought perhaps she had calmed, but then Betty cocked her arm and flung it forward, slapping Josie's cheek with the slipper's thin plastic sole hard enough to cause a sharp, stinging pain.

"Get out!" she said, and then she pushed Josie's tray to the floor, where it clattered and broke.

———◦———

Louise was called. "Mother," she tried to reason, "Josie is here to help. Surely you remember – Jim's partner in New York told us about her. She took care of his children for more than ten years, and he says she is very trustworthy – and gentle and honest and good."

Betty said nothing.

"You mustn't hit her, mother," Louise continued.

"I don't like her face," Betty said.

"Mom!" Louise cried. "Mom, please! Please can't you at least try to be kind?"

It was a question that Louise must long have wished to ask, ever since the day that Betty had declared her too old for dolls, and dismembered her favorites into the rag bin; ever since the day, as a teen, when she mustered the nerve to tell her parents that she wished to be a architect, and to build great palaces in the sky — not statehouses or stately homes, but low income housing where those who did not have could unpack their secrets, and unfurl their dreams. This ambition, once confessed, was defeated by a frown and a shake of her mother's head that could hardly be called such, so quickly and effortlessly had it been made.

It was a logical question, but one that would not do, because Betty existed now in a world outside of reason, and outside of ordinary time. She lived inside a season of resurrected memories—memories of days spent in Grandma Alice's kitchen, watching her make rhubarb pies and stuffed quahogs so rich and buttery that the clams might be imagined to have sacrificed themselves willingly to the delight. Baby Betty, as she was known then, sat on a step ladder and listened while Grandma Alice talked—she gossiped and quoted scripture, which were well-nigh the same, in Alice's handling of them. Later Betty was given rolling pins and measuring spoons to play with, and eventually small jobs: trimming the pie crust and shaking the cinnamon sugar over the scraps and rolling them so that even these could be baked, because nothing was ever allowed to go to waste—not so much as a single minute wherein Grandma Alice could gather Baby Betty inside her soft and steadfast love.

———◆———

The next morning Betty knocked her oatmeal to the floor, and the morning after that Josie prepared creamy soft-boiled eggs and fresh berries in a bowl. Betty examined this bounty for a minute, and then she lifted Grandma Alice's prized cut-glass saltshaker from the table and threw it against the far front porch window. The window was tempered and did not break, but the salt shaker shattered when it hit the ground, sending facets and damp sticky salt to all four corners of the porch.

Betty fell to her knees and crawled across the porch towards the worst of the mess; she swept at it with her hands, gathering the shards together and cutting her palms. She ground salt into these wounds with each pass of her hands across the floor.

"I'm sorry, Grandma Alice," she said. "I'm sorry... "

Josie disappeared and returned with a dustpan and broom.

"Grandma Alice, she say never mind. She say we sweep together, and that you still her sweet girl."

"Grandma Alice?"

"Grandma Alice, she say me all that and more besides. She say we sweep and then we make fresh eggs. Grandma Alice say only hot eggs good enough for sweet girl. But first she say we wash you hands. Come, Ma'am Betty," she said, extending her hands towards the old woman on the floor.

Betty looked at Josie for a long minute, and did not move. After a time, Josie reached down and took her by her frail forearms, so as to spare her cut palms. "Come, Ma'am Betty. Come. I am Josie, and Grandma Alice say you let me take you good care."

———⋅◉⋅———

When Louise stopped by later that day, Josie had her shopping list all ready. Chocolate pudding, it read. Chocolate ice cream, whipped cream and strawberries. The makings for angel food cake. Ham, white bread and American cheese. Real mayonnaise and potato chips. Louise raised her eyebrows. "Ma'am Betty, she itchy," Josie said.

"Tell me about it," Louise replied.

"Maybe you find something soft for she wear – like the kids. Ai-yah, how you say–a sweat suit."

"She won't wear it," Louise answered.

"Still, maybe you find."

After lunch, Betty dozed for a few minutes. When she woke, she looked at Josie and said, "I thought I'd like to take my walk."

"Come, Ma'am Betty," Josie said. "We go."

I was elated the first time I saw the two out strolling along the beach road, and I was even happier to notice, after the passing of several weeks, that Betty appeared to have put on a few pounds. And then I saw something that made me sit up rather straighter indeed.

After Betty's lunch on a rainy day, when there could be no walk, Josie said, "Come, Ma'am Betty. I take you care." Josie stretched out her hand and Betty took it; Josie led her up the stairs and into the pink-tiled bathroom. She sat Betty in her bath chair in the old stall shower and wrapped an old pink towel around her shoulders. She adjusted the temperature to a soothing degree and pulled the retractable hose from its faucet. She washed the old woman's hair and then gently she toweled it dry. Patiently, then, she rummaged through closets and cabinets until she found what she was looking for: an old hair dryer that she set to low, and a soft bristled brush. With infinite care she dried Betty's thin, downy hair.

In the vanity, under the sink, she found some long-forgotten rollers and a few old pins. She lifted Betty out of the bath chair, and helped her to dress in the soft cottons that Louise had delivered the week before. Then she led Betty back down the stairs and seated her in a soft chair on the porch. "I style you now, Ma'am Betty," she said, and the old woman closed her eyes. Josie set the rollers and pins at arms length on the rickety, ancient porch table that Betty had been unwilling to part with, even at Harold's urging, and began to set the old woman's hair.

Betty dozed, and when she woke Josie gentled the pins and rollers from the old woman's hair, careful not to pull it. She brushed the tight curls into soft waves that framed Betty's face, and then she stood back to take a look. In the deep crevasses on the old lady's face, she saw the rugged hillsides of her youth. In Betty's milky eyes, she saw her sisters, naked and playing in the surf on a litter-strewn beach. The breeze brought the sound of the Pacific, the ocean of her childhood—she held up a long-handled hand mirror. "Look, Ma'am Betty. See? You beautiful."

———

The next morning Louise came over to find her mother sitting on the basement steps, watching Josie fold laundry. She had been impelled, apparently, by the soft sound of Josie's singing, which wafted through the house. Her voice rose exultant and full of hope, and in a language none of us knew. Each time Josie sang the hymn through, Betty asked her to begin over new, and always Josie obliged. Nevertheless, Louise was appalled to find her mother in so precarious a spot. Louise descended a few steps and held out her hand.

"Mother, please, get up," she said.

But Betty waved her away. "I'm fine here, dear," she said. "Just fine."

"Mother, your hair. It's lovely," Louise said, noticing. "And there's something else..."

"Yes, it is a bit of alright, isn't it, dear?" Betty said, running a light hand across her forehead. And then she gestured towards the step beside her. "Have a seat?"

———

It was, perhaps, my imagination, but it seemed to me that Louise's visits became more frequent from that point forward—and that at times she chose to linger. On occasion I even noticed her out along the beach road, keeping slow pace with Betty and Josie as they poked along. When the weather was fine and the windows could be opened, Josie's singing would come to me, the same hymn over and again: haunting, because I could not place it.

Betty died last year, uneventfully, in her sleep. Prudence and common courtesy both required that she provide some inkling as to her wishes, and this she had done. In the top drawer of her mother's nightstand, Louise found a yellowed envelope with her name printed neatly across the front. Beneath her name, also printed neatly, were the words "To be opened upon my death." Inside the envelope was a note.

Dear Louise,

Not wishing to be remiss in any way, this note contains a few instructions regarding my arrangements. Although the church has not amounted to much in my life, I must say that Reverend Veith up to the Congregational did a fine job after Harold's passing, so should you wish there to be a formal service of any sort, please do contact him. As I am sure you are aware, your father and I were married in that church, so I suppose a little something there might be fitting, all things considered.

At present I have no special requests for hymns or readings. And please tell Reverend Veith he needn't fuss over my eulogy. Tell him I'd like it known that I always tried to do my best—that is sufficient for me.

As for my remains, please do not bury me—I simply couldn't bear it. I wish to be cremated, and for my ashes to be scattered at the high point of the bluff across the street. In death, if not in life, I wish to ride the wind and waves as far as they will take me.

There were no more than a dozen of us in church on the day of Betty's funeral—Louise and Jim, their children, and Josie, too, of course. I was there, along with a few old friends of Harold's—those who could still drive—and a cousin on her mother's side. Carol, Louise's younger sister, had phoned to say she couldn't get away.

Louise took the pulpit; she stood still there for several minutes—composing herself, I surmised—but then a few more minutes ticked by, and Jim stood up and began to move towards her. "No, no—I'm alright," she said, stepping down from the pulpit and towards the small altar which held Betty's ashes and a stand of framed photos. Louise stood behind the altar and rested her hands lightly upon it. "I'd be lying if I told you how wonderful my mother always was—how maternal and loving and full of life. Because all of you know—she wasn't easy. I mean, she's dead so I guess I can finally just go ahead and say it—she could be pretty mean. But after Josie came she was different somehow, nicer. I wish now I'd had longer to get to know her..." It was then that Jim went to her, wrapped his arm around her and led her back to their pew. He is a dear boy.

———————

That was a year ago, give or take, and it was just last week that Louise told us it was time. She gathered us together and then motioned for us to stay, so Josie, Jim and I stood in the deep shade, the maple's holy branches strong and spread wide above us, while she crossed the street and scrambled up the bluff, the sun hot and strong above her. She cradled the small box for a moment, and then she lifted the lid. After some interval of time—seconds, an hour, it is impossible to say—a gust came, and Louise tilted the box in the direction of the water, and that fast it was done. And then she crossed the road back towards us, and we stood together under the tree—the magnificent gift of some long-ago planter—and we toasted to Betty with the white Zinfandel she loved.

———◦———

I have begun to forget things, just small things here and there, so Josie lives with me now. "Ai-yah, Ma'am Ruth. You naughty!" Josie scolded when she caught on, and I suppose perhaps I am. For it is, after all, wrong to interfere, and yet this is precisely what I did on the day I plied Jim with lobster. He had, you see, once made mention once of a domestic who continued to live-in with a colleague of his although their need for her had long been outgrown. "It's crazy. Really crazy," he had said. "Guy still pays her and everything. Says she was the answer to a prayer he didn't know how to pray — whatever that means."

"Track her down," I told him, wiping my mouth. "Today."

On my best days, I'd have planted seeds, and smiled to watch the idea grow into Jim's very own. But after Betty's retrieval by the police, it was obvious I no longer had that kind of time.

We sit on my porch now, Josie and I. She tells me her stories and I tell her mine. And we watch the water rise and recede, rise and recede, grinding even the hardest granite to dust.

The Zen Art of Peeling Potatoes

By Edda R. Pitassi

It was a fine June afternoon, and Lori decided to call Joyce before starting Sunday dinner. Joyce's recent news of another spike in her sugar level worried Lori. At the same time, she felt exhausted knowing she had to muster enough adrenalin to keep them both engaged in upbeat conversation.

She dialed the familiar number.

"Hi, Joyce."

Lori listened sympathetically as Joyce reported levels passing the dangerous 400 number in her ongoing battle with diabetes. Lori read somewhere on the Internet that diabetes chose only beautiful, talented, intelligent women to wreak its havoc. This was Joyce.

Lori offered a few helpful remarks about diet.

"I know…I know," Joyce laughed. "I'm staying away from the pasta and concentrating on the veggies."

They decided to talk again in a few days. As Lori placed the receiver in its slot on the wall, she couldn't help wondering *why*.

Why do we stay connected?

Although they had a long history as friends, their telephone conversations were sporadic at best. Actually, Lori had three best friends: Cora, Mary, and Joyce. They had known each other for over four decades, and their efforts at keeping the friendships ongoing sometimes seemed uncoordinated or clumsy. Yet they never strayed from a small, inner voice they each kept close inside, like a needle on a compass, pointing to who they once were and where they came from.

Walking over to the sink, Lori rinsed the potatoes for dinner that night. She was learning to focus on the holiness of the ordinary and the routine as she grew older, and as she reflected upon her life. The cool water on her hands felt soothing. She was determined to practice the simple Zen spirituality of taking one raw potato at a time, peeling it, slicing it, and placing the portions in a bowl of cold water.

<hr />

However dispirited her life and those of her friends had become, Lori knew she could not turn away from a relationship that began when she, Joyce, Cora, and Mary had been secure, bubbly, outgoing twenty- and thirty-something single working girls. How caught up they all had been in the '60s and '70s backdrop of "The Mary Tyler Moore Show" and "That Girl" — those popular, single-female-centered TV shows — and the sweeping feminist and liberation themes of their generation.

Products of Roman Catholic educations — and living at home with mothers, fathers, sisters, and brothers — Lori and her friends enjoyed the chance to be part of the growing singles scene in Philadelphia and its suburbs. They went to their office jobs during the day, attended evening college courses two to three times a week, and hit the popular bar scene most Wednesday nights, searching for the excitement of the

Marlo Thomas character, "Ann Marie." That iconic lifestyle teased, tantalized, and tempted four virgins.

They were not pining for marriage. But they did have infatuations and a yearning for romance. They sought to meet men at work, night school, a political rally, or on a beach at the South Jersey Shore. Such encounters started to define the direction they would eventually take as single, married, and divorced women.

Their paths toward nuptial bliss suffered more than a few wrong turns over the years. Lori felt they often left things unsaid because they did not want to expose, or confess, their naiveté to one another. Or maybe, she mused, rinsing another potato, the anxiety and regret over failed romance disappointed and hurt too much to share.

There were other more subtle motives, perhaps. A mother's determined desire to keep her daughter close, safe, secure — and unmarried — proved more than Cora wanted to discuss. Maybe Lori herself should have insisted *no* when her own ailing 75-year-old mother swayed her, at the age of fifty and against her own better judgment, to marry Greg.

However, that was yesterday, and yesterday was gone. She started to hum the tune from the 1963 Chad & Jeremy song, "Yesterday's Gone;" she paused peeling. The unhurried pace of her task continued to loosen tightly held memories that Lori had confined to a corner of time long ago. It was typical of her to get nostalgic on Sundays, remembering family dinners in her South Philadelphia row home, summer weekends at the shore, her close relationship with her younger sister, Amy, who died of breast cancer at thirty.

Yes, she thought. *Of course, that's a big part of our connection all these years. Amy's illness left its mark on our tight foursome. Amy's sense of humor and dry wit was an integral part of our delight in being young, single and unencumbered, of having any and all possibilities.*

In December 1974, two months before her 31st birthday, Amy had come into Lori's bedroom one night. Amy was looking forward to moving out and had already put a down payment on an affordable Center City apartment. She had unbuttoned her pajama top and said, "Look."

Lori stared at a mass of lumpy skin on Amy's right breast. She raised her fingers to touch it and felt the uneven, swollen bump.

"Amy," she said, "How long has this been here?"

Amy said she had watched it get to its present size since the summer.

"And you didn't tell anybody?" All at once, Lori felt dizzy and sweaty. "Why didn't you tell me sooner? We have to see a doctor right away."

At that moment, they both looked at each other, tears in their eyes, and Lori said what she was trying to keep inside.

"How do we tell Mom and Dad, Amy? How do we tell them?"

Lori, Cora, Joyce and Mary grew up the day Amy died. It had been a humid, rainy day in the summer of 1977.

Amy's death haunted them that summer. Stunned and unable to put their grief aside, they avoided driving to their favorite South Jersey spot, Avalon, with its memories of carefree weekends on the beach.

They talked about NBC News correspondent, Betty Rollin, and her bestselling book, *First, You Cry*, about her battle with breast cancer. They called their doctors and asked about mammograms and were told, "At thirty, unless there's a family history of cancer, you're too young to be screened."

They breathed sighs of relief. Lori went forward later that year for her first screening.

She would learn after her only sister's death how the sorrow of a child's illness and death lingers over a home and never really leaves the minds and hearts of loving parents. She could still remember her mother's swollen and vacant eyes the days and weeks after the funeral. She could recall her outgoing, gregarious father dial a close family member and choke up as he reported the news of his daughter's death.

Lori glimpses her sister's photograph every day, displayed as it is next to her parents' picture in her living room. Over the years, she felt her sister's passing slowly fade into memory. She never allowed herself to get weepy in the company of her friends, believing that it was more adult to accept the hurt.

———◦◦◦———

Suddenly, now, she noticed her wrinkly hands next to the smooth, newly peeled potato. She enjoyed the water's way of slowly, softly passing through her fingers. She sighed, shook her head, and continued to think about her friends.

While Joyce and Mary eventually married, Lori always felt closer to Cora, probably because they were single and professionals longer than the other two.

She paused at the sink and recalled a recent telephone conversation with Cora.

"Hi, how are things going these days?" Lori had asked.

"Okay, I guess. Same old, same old. I wake up with all these aches and pains. Thank god for hot showers in the morning."

Cora continues to fight weight gain. She dresses stylishly and, like the rest of them, colors her hair, which is now a warm, reddish-brown shade that enhances both her enormous brown eyes and lovely skin. Even at the tender age of sixty-five, Cora still turns heads when she enters a room.

Cora dated a lot over the 40 years they had known each other, but one man – Ted – was the romance that stood out.

As Lori remembered him, Ted was not the professional career type. He worked with his hands, outdoors, engineering and installing underground gas pipelines. Her mind took her back to a day when Lori, Cora and Cora's mother stood in Cora's living room getting ready for a shopping trip and movie.

"You're not moving to Kentucky with him, are you?" Without waiting for an answer, Cora's mom persisted with her own storyline. "It's too far, and he can't provide what you've been used to."

Cora offered no response. She simply walked to the front door, waited for Lori to step out first, and closed the door behind them. They walked to Cora's car. Lori delayed a bit at her passenger side, expecting Cora to say something – anything – about what had just happened. Instead, Cora talked about their jobs, new clothes, and where to eat lunch. There was no mention of Ted. As usual, Lori didn't press.

Lori knew that Cora's mom fully expected her daughter to marry well. A suit and a tie, genteel manners, security, and money were essentials to securing the American Dream. Lori never heard or saw Cora cry about missing Ted when the affair ended, even though he married someone else soon after.

Lori kept quiet, fearful that offering any observations about the relationship between Cora and her mother might upset her friend.

That week when they had talked on the phone, Lori and Cora discussed a possible time and place to meet with Joyce and Mary. They decided on their favorite Italian bistro. Then Cora veered off into her usual pessimism. After a fall in her home a few years ago, Cora had started looking into a variety of retirement communities.

"I'm by myself," she told Lori. "I have no one to care for me. I discovered that after my accident on the stairs."

Lori listened to her friend's complaints. She wanted to scream.

You let your mom run your life. You did not follow your heart with Ted when you should have. Now you're alone . . . financially secure, but alone. This is what happens when you don't take a chance at life. . .when you don't roll the dice. You remember the lyrics of "Ruby Tuesday," don't you? 'Catch your dreams before they slip away. . .Ain't life unkind.'

She wanted to scream! *Life isn't perfect!*

———◦◦◦———

As she peeled potatoes and thought about that conversation, Lori realized how all of them had suffered letdowns and disillusionment.

The year was 1980, and Lori was heading out the door to her new corporate job when Cora called.

"Joyce is giving Rich the boot. He says Joyce can't seem to drop the pounds fast enough for him. He leaves notes about her weight gain all over the house. He's so into fitness, you know. I think the last straw was the note he left for Joyce on the bathroom wall before he went to work last week," Cora said.

"C'mon," Lori said. "He knew when they married she wasn't a carpenter's dream. I cannot believe they can't work this out. How silly. And the baby isn't even two years old yet."

Lori watched the sun cast its late afternoon shade over the deck, and wondered if Joyce's life might have been happier had she remarried after the divorce. She had belonged to a community theater group where she met and dated several men. Nothing more serious than friendship ever came of it.

Now, Joyce lives with her 33-year-old son, Colin. He works on-line from his home computer, although Lori suspects he spends his days aimlessly trolling the Internet. Several years ago, something happened to his leg or his foot or his back, but Joyce doesn't talk much about it. She hints he receives some type of government assistance. To supplement their income, Joyce drives to work Monday through Friday to a part-time job. Lori thinks it valiant because her friend walks with a cane after a nasty fall two years ago.

Joyce never says whether Colin drives her to work. She confided that her son's goal is to become a male model.

———⊙———

As another potato finds its way to Lori's hand, she watches her life and the lives of her friends pass in front of her mind's eye. One particular telephone conversation she had years ago with Cora about Mary's shaky marriage stands out.

"Did you hear that John is now drinking more than usual? How is Mary going to deal with this?"

The four of them decided to meet for a Saturday breakfast at a nearby diner. That's when Mary confessed her marriage was over. A terrible sadness came over Mary's delicate face.

All Lori could think was, *how could John be so reckless. . .so out of control?*

"We went to the doctor, and it's John who can't have children. It's not me. He's not taking the news well."

John kept working at his family's business. He kept drinking. He came home later and later. Mary kept working, and then she found out he cheated. Some ten years into her marriage, she eventually filed for divorce.

A few weeks ago, Lori found herself on the phone with Mary, who used the word *trapped* more than once. Mary's 93-year-old mother died two years ago, leaving Mary and her sister, Chloe, alone together for the first time in their lives. They had cared for their mother, living on a mish-mash of her Social Security checks, Chloe's disability coverage and additional SSI checks. These helped pay the monthly mortgage payments and grocery bills. Chloe, who never worked due to ongoing mental health problems throughout her life, attempted suicide over a year ago by overdosing on pain medications.

Now Mary is retired, keeps looking for part-time work, and has had to dip into her retirement account. She had suffered a nasty concussion when a speeding cyclist knocked her down as she stood waiting to cross a street. Mary doesn't always remember facts and dates.

All of them were persevering in their individual struggles to keep their edge. . .to keep away from the edge.

Lately, Lori worries about her own life, about having enough savings to see her and her husband, Greg, through retirement, monthly mortgage payments, illness, and aging.

When they started dating in the mid-1980s, Lori fell hard for his endearing British accent and big blue eyes. She knew he was unconventional – an original jack-of-all-trades, master of many – competent, skilled, practical. Throughout their romance, that added to his appeal. She also knew he had been married twice before.

Today, Lori admits that she lives with a classic eccentric: intelligent, intensely curious and opinionated.

When friends ask, "How's Greg doing after his heart attack?" Lori tells them that he hasn't stopped smoking, that he's remarkably fit considering what he went through last year, and that his legs ache most times. She tries to stay upbeat.

Instead of abiding by doctor's orders to walk a mile every day, he chooses to work on cars. Twisting his slim, wiry torso, he slides under car engines and repairs some mechanical malfunction or patches a damaged front bumper.

"This is not what the doctor suggested as exercise," she shouts from the deck and begs him to stop.

They bicker. She backs away, fearing that her wifely advice will upset him and cause another attack. As she prepares their Sunday dinner, Lori observes him moving a few chairs on the deck.

Greg, the man she married 20 years ago, never overcame the loss of his consulting job soon after they first met. He never found another steady line of work. Too proud for his own good, he didn't seem to benefit much from a six-month stint with a skilled marriage counselor they had gone to for help ten years ago.

When they lived together in her small home in the late 1980s, they were not married, as he was waiting for his final divorce papers. She was in love with him but wasn't sure about marriage. She loved her job, loved being with her friends, and enjoyed painting and fixing up her small, suburban Cape Cod.

Then her mother fell down a flight of stairs at home, and Lori began a dizzying life of keeping doctors' appointments, staying with her mother several nights a week, driving back and forth between houses on weekends, and all the while trying to look professional and calm at the office. When her mom experienced a series of strokes, her employer allowed her to go to a four-day week. She and Greg brought Mom to live with them. He remained by her side through all the turmoil.

After visiting several vascular specialists, all the doctors agreed her mother required aortic bifemoral bypass surgery - an extensive procedure to address the pain and weakness from iliac disease in her legs - or risk amputation of her leg.

After her mother's surgery, she and Greg found an Italian-speaking companion who stayed with her mom during the day. They took over at night. This went on for several months. Confined to a wheelchair, her mother asked when she and Greg would marry.

"Mama, I don't want to get married," she repeatedly told her mother.

To lessen the sadness in her mother's face, and in the middle of a massive layoff at her job, she and Greg applied for a marriage license. In early July 1992, a minister married them in her home. Cora, Mary, and Joyce and a few family members celebrated with them.

By the end of July that same year, she and 55,000 corporate employees worldwide lost their jobs. In mid-September, she cradled her dying mother in her arms, called her "Mama" one last time, and watched her take her last breath. Greg was by her side.

———◦———

Lori let out a deep sigh and returned to the final touches to her dinner preparation. She called out to Greg. "Get ready. Dinner will be on the table in ten minutes."

Quickly moving about to arrange forks and knives, she appreciated the calm refuge and stillness of this extraordinary Sunday with its perfect light and evening breeze.

Thinking about long friendships – and viewing her own untidy and imperfect life – focused her mind. However, she was realistic enough not to expect her quiet meditations would put an end to the fears and worries she and her friends were living through.

On balance, she had to admit that peeling potatoes – with cool water softly passing through her fingers – helped.

Aging

Remembering Jean, My Mentor and Confidante

By Lynda M. Clemens

The night is chillier than normal for early September, with a faint crescent moon hung high in the sky. A damp breeze blows in from the river, and Jean wraps her thin sweater closer to her body. She keeps moving along in the dark, tripping over the rough untended ground. *Where's the house? Where's Fisher's Lane?* She repeats to herself over and over. *Why can't I see Sears?*

She stumbles onto the train tracks. *I can follow these home. I can get to Sears. I'm not lost like Dad always was. Dad . . . what happened to him? I can't remember. He could never remember a thing either. I'm getting just like him.*

A light appears in the distance, wobbling like a handheld flashlight might. *Is Dad coming for me?* She thinks as the light approaches, getting bigger and brighter, with a rumbling noise. Dad . . . she sees him lying still in the casket; her weeping sister stands nearby. *Dad, you must be in heaven . . . and I don't have to get like you.*

She opens her arms and moves toward the light.

———◦◦◦———

Jean – a kind of second mother to me. Jean – a reading buddy. Jean – my mother-in-law. It's hard for me to believe she has been gone 25 years. I'm about Jean's age now and, when she died, I made a vow. It's time I honor that vow. It's time to tell her story...our story.

———◦◦◦———

I've imagined Jean's final moments on this earth many times since that call from Karen 25 years ago, telling me her mother's broken body had been found lying near the tracks where she was hit by a passing train. She had wandered away, somehow, when her husband, Jack, had gone to the bathroom at one of the football season's first Eagles home games at Vets' Stadium. (If you're from Philly, it is *Vets'* not *Veterans*)

Slowly – over several years - Jean's memory and thought processes had been failing. Since she could speak, attend to basic personal grooming, and often portray her old self for short periods of time, she might be diagnosed today in the mild phase of early onset Alzheimer's disease.

The last time I saw Jean, in August 1986, I had just moved back to Pennsylvania from California with my second husband, John. The biggest irony of my life is that Dave and I divorced after ten years because I was unwilling, no, in truth, unable to be more like his mother. I was pleased that Jean recognized me then, but unfortunately she could not remember my name. She followed the conversation she, Jack, and I were having, but made few comments. I kissed her goodbye and Jack walked me to my car.

Turning to him, I asked, "Does Jean know what is happening to her?"

He explained that Jean had been given the full diagnosis and prognosis and, at that time two years ago, understood the implications. He said she brought up her father's illness to the doctor, asking him if the same thing would happen to her.

"Each Alzheimer's patient is different, and no one can predict the exact course the disease would take," said the doctor.

I couldn't help but think that perhaps, like many care-giving families, Jean's family overestimated her health and abilities. I certainly believed that Jack would never have left her alone in her stadium seat for even five minutes if he knew her decline was worsening.

———◦———

We grew up in Frankford, one of many Philadelphia neighborhoods, in a city renowned as the City of Neighborhoods, in the post-WWII era, when kids still organized their own sports. Summers we would disappear after breakfast and reach home just in time for dinner. Lunch was provided by the nearest mother – usually just peanut and jelly sandwiches, as we were middle class, hardly affluent. My secret preference was to lunch with Mrs. B, as we all called Jean back then.

"We" were a bunch of kids from four different families who, more or less, depending on ages and age-appropriate activities, hung out together. We all participated in church choir, the Christmas pageant, Sunday school and, of course, weekly church services.

We piled in or behind Mrs. B's pew, where she would hand out peppermints to keep us quiet during the erudite sermons from our pontificating, Princeton-educated, minister. After all, what teen or pre-teen is enthralled with citations from Greek, Latin and German texts, in the original languages, no less?

A thin, very short, birdlike woman, Jean would cock her head just like a wren when listening to you, locking eyes and smiling. She seldom wore lipstick or other makeup but was vain enough to dye her hair when the gray started to appear. She stayed at home doing all those '50s and '60s things women were expected to do. She loved to bake and generously taught me how.

College educated with a degree in English, she had worked at some clerical jobs briefly until marrying Jack Brown after the war and dutifully having three children. David came first, then Gary and, after a seven year hiatus, the longed for daughter, Karen.

Dave would, at the tender age of 20, become my first husband. Marriage was expected after our high school courtship, especially when Jean found out we were, heaven forbid, sleeping together.

Mrs. B was an active volunteer, especially for the Presbyterian Church of Frankford we all attended. Voracious readers, she and I would often share our latest finds, especially as I got older. We never tired of discussing *Gone With the Wind*, *Forever Amber* or *Anna Karenina*.

I still laugh about a disagreement we had over Tolstoy's famous quote on happy and unhappy families. I was taking a required formal logic class at LaSalle College night school and kept arguing that if there were many reasons families were unhappy, there had to be many reasons families were happy. Mrs. B just held her ground, saying when I got as old as she was, I just might have changed my mind about that. She was right, as usual, but now I can't tell her so.

Like the best of TV moms, she had the ability to offer sound advice and wise insights without alienating us . . . sort of like June Cleaver, sans the pearls and fancy dresses.

Mr. B, or Jack, was the Comptroller of Friends' Hospital in Northeast Philadelphia where they lived, over the years, in two different, but equally lovely, stone houses on the grounds. Thanks to Jean and Jack's living situation, we all had access to the extensive gardens, ball fields, tennis courts, snack bar and other patient amenities.

Friends' Hospital, the oldest private psychiatric hospital in the country, was founded by Quakers in 1813 and remains world-renowned for providing a more humane treatment of the mentally ill. The celebrated azalea gardens are still open to the public every spring, and I often go there to visit. Friends' prides itself on innovative approaches to therapy and involves the patients in the care of the gardens.

Of course, there were also the patients themselves to manage. We were expected to be respectful and polite to them. I remember Clem, an unfortunate victim of the early 1950s lobotomy craze before his 21st birthday. When I first met him in the snack bar, he had been at Friends' for decades. He seldom spoke and walked the grounds in good weather, sweet but with a vacant look in his eyes. He just smoked his pipe, stopping to admire the azaleas and the myriad of other flowers.

I learned sympathy and tolerance for those troubled souls, just as the Quakers' mission statement hoped. When I had to decide on a college major, I think my experiences at Friends' contributed to my choice of psychology.

The Browns' first house was located on Fisher's Lane across the street from a golf course with enough of a hill to satisfy our early sledding needs. Later, with Jack's promotions, they would move to a larger residence, closer to the main buildings of the hospital. We would sled and roll in the snow until wet and tired and then descend on Mrs. B. We knew she would have cocoa and homemade cookies waiting for us. No one was chastised for wet boots on her kitchen floor or other messes, for that matter. It was as if she welcomed, or at least tolerated, these unavoidable trappings of wet, snowy days. We were like an extended family, with Mrs. B nudging us, by words and example, toward adulthood.

I remember one winter day, when I was twelve, taking leave from the rest of the sledding party to help Mrs. B with the cookies. I loved the smell of the baking sweets and the cocoa on the back burner of the stove, but I had an ulterior motive. I needed to talk about my stepfather.

Pulling a tray from the oven, I broached the subject. "Mrs. B, I need to tell you something." I averted my face from her gaze.

"Slide those cookies onto this rack and then sit down," Mrs. B replied. "Milk or cocoa?"

I stared into my cup of cocoa, not knowing where to begin. "Remember I told you Fred, my stepdad, would grab and tickle me when I was a kid until I was beside myself crying on the floor?"

"Yes, I remember." Mrs. B acknowledged, pouring milk in her coffee. "Once you told your mother how much you hated it, it stopped, right?"

"Yeah but now he's coming into my room in the middle of the night, flicking the overhead light on and off. He's drunk and Mom's asleep," I confided.

"Have you told your mom?"

"I can't. They fight all the time now. This would be just one more topic to scream about. What if they get a divorce? I'm scared."

"You really need to tell your mother. This is not normal and I'm worried for you," she said.

"What do you mean?"

Mrs. B sighed and did not flinch as she leaned across the table. "Well, as girls get older and start to develop, some men, especially if they are not true relatives, get excited by it and want to see more. Sometimes they even want to touch the girl. You wouldn't like that, I can tell. I need you to tell your mom, or I will have to."

I burst into tears and sobbed, "You mean like those naked women in that magazine I found in the basement? I can't tell her. If they break up, we'll have no place to go. My brother's only five years old."

She walked over to me, leaned over, and put her arm around my shoulder. Looking me in the eyes, she said, "Will you promise to tell me or your mom if this keeps up or gets worse? Can you wear pjs and top and bottom underwear so there's less for him to see? This isn't going to stop, especially since he drinks. I know about drunks, my dear. I tended my mother for many years, often having to put her to bed, due to her alcohol problems. It's no excuse, but you need to understand his drinking removes what little control of his behavior he may have."

I drew breath, sobbed again and then hiccupped. Finally, I got it out.

"I promise. I know it isn't good or right, but I can't tell mom right now."

Calmer, I mustered up a wicked little grin. "I think I'll jump up and run toward their bedroom calling Mom. That might scare him off."

Mrs. B cupped my face and gently wiped away the last tears.

———◈———

If Jean had grit, she also had wit. I not only witnessed one of Jean's spontaneous comic assaults, I got dragged in to help. Dave loved a worn black shirt with a red paisley design. It had been through the wash so many times; the elbows were like tissue paper and the black almost gray. Mrs. B made constant disparaging remarks about this situation, but Dave ignored her. One afternoon, Dave and I arrived at his house, having taken buses together from The Philadelphia High School for Girls, a.k.a. Girls' High, and the all male Central High, located only a block apart. Dave was wearing "the shirt."

"Come here, dear," said Mrs. B.

Suspicious of her tone, Dave headed for the stairs with Jean in hot pursuit. Sticking out her finger, she caught the new hole she had spied. Pulling down, she wrenched the left sleeve partially off his arm.

"Come on Lynda, help me!" she urged with a laugh. Together we had the whole shirt in tatters in no time at all. Dave played along beautifully when the door opened and Jack walked in from work.

"Dad, Dad, you've got to save me" cried Dave, melodramatically clinging to the newel post.

"Save yourself, son. You know I don't cross your mother."

———— ◆ ————

Mrs. B's kitchen was always a magnet for the family and all visitors. A large room in the converted mill they first lived in on Fisher's Lane, it seemed to be in use every waking hour. In addition to the standard uses for cooking and eating, the Brown's kitchen table witnessed endless board games in the '50s, resounding teens vs. adults political debates in the '60s, and card games too numerous to count. I learned to play bridge there after Dave and I got engaged. It seems that skill was prerequisite for joining the family.

In the spring of my junior year at Girls' High, I remember flying into Mrs. B's kitchen like the devil was behind, throwing myself into a chair, unable to say a word. I'd run close to a mile from the bus stop. Panting, I finally asked if she had the news on.

"No. Why?"

"She's dead and I saw it." I croaked.

"Who's dead? What are you talking about?" she asked, her voice cracking in dismay.

Taking deep breaths, I explained that I was sitting by the window in hygiene class looking out over the playing fields, not paying much attention in the last period of the day. Hockey practice was all I was thinking about when a body flew past the window right in front of my eyes. I screamed, of course, and jumped up to the window where I saw the crumpled body in the stairwell by the gym. The teacher immediately forced us all back to our seats.

"They came on the loud speaker in about five minutes and said there had been a tragic accident and we were all to get our things and go home immediately. School and all after-school activities were suspended."

Jean and I moved to the living room and turned on the television. After about half an hour, a special bulletin alert flashed across the screen. They showed a female reporter standing on the front steps of Girls' High describing how a student had fallen in a tragic accident. The student was dead, but no name would be released at this time. There were no details to report yet as the police were just starting to investigate how the student had gotten access to the roof of the school, the reporter said. Mrs. B and I looked at each other too stunned to speak.

School resumed the next day, but it was close to a week before the newspapers and rumor mill started to jive. I think Lauren's younger sister, who also attended Girls', was the source of most details. The story that got pieced together was that Lauren, a senior who I didn't know personally, was pregnant. Afraid to tell her parents, she gained access to the roof of the school and jumped.

Mrs. B and I were alone in the kitchen when I told her why the girl had committed suicide.

"How could she kill herself?" I whispered, wiping away the tears.

"Sure it was bad, sure her parents would freak out, but to die over a stupid mistake? I'd never, ever do something so stupid."

Mrs. B paused for a long time. "Lynda, you should never say never. Who knows why someone makes such a choice. I think if things were bad enough, I might want to end it rather than fight on."

"You? You have to be kidding me. Don't you know how feisty everyone considers you to be? Between your brains, humor and sheer guts, you intimidate just about everyone. That's why you mostly get your way," I blurted.

"That may be," she laughed, then grew very serious, "but I'm not feisty enough for some things life throws our way."

<hr />

Mrs. B's Scottish dad, Grandpa McKay, visited from upstate New York every summer for a minimum of two weeks. Jean dreaded, as well as longed for, these visits. Every year his memory seemed worse, and she would complain that he just wasn't paying enough attention.

"How," she would ask, throwing her frustration out into the air or to anyone who would listen, "can someone not remember what they did this very morning?"

"How can a grandfather forget the simplest facts about his only grandchildren?"

"How can Grandpa not know that you turn left to get to Sears, when the clock tower is visible from the house, for heaven's sake?"

I was stirring some gravy for Sunday dinner when Mrs. B's sister called. I had met Janice at our wedding and did not really know her since she and her husband lived in upstate New York near Grandpa. Jean answered the phone in the hallway. Of course I only heard one side of the conversation, but the meaning was clear.

"What do you mean you're looking into homes for him? . . . Of course I know that you are the one dealing with it day in and day out . . . I'll ask Jack to get the name of an expert from work . . . Maybe you all can come down and get a second opinion. Maybe there are some new breakthroughs on dementia."

"I'm sorry, Sis. I really didn't think it was that bad. I guess peeing and pooping himself is the last straw. No, I don't blame you. I wish you had told me sooner, but no one is blaming you. I'll call as soon as Jack has an expert's name. Love ya, kid. Bye."

———— ◦◦◦ ————

About eight years into our marriage, Dave and I were sitting around the fire at the Brown's new home on the Friends' Hospital grounds facing Roosevelt Boulevard. Karen was home from college. Jean was perusing a magazine, slowly turning pages with no visible interest. I had my nose in a book, as usual, while the others watched tv.

The phone rang around 8 o'clock. Jean picked up the receiver. She listened but said little. She hung up after about five minutes.

"That was Gary," she said.

"What did he say? Is Eunice in labor? Is everything okay? Is the baby here already?"

We chorused our questions at her, excited about her first grandchild.

Jean just stared at us mutely for some time, shaking her head. She kept her hand on the receiver and looked again at the phone as if the answers would come to her.

"I don't know. I don't know. I don't remember . . ."

This was the very first indication that something was happening to Jean. We didn't realize it at the time, assuming she was so excited, she just failed to process what Gary was telling her.

Jean's funeral service was at our church, of course. Two of the choir's soloists, a lyric bass-baritone and a thrilling contralto, brought the entire congregation to tears with their tribute to Jean. A long, long cortège slowly drove to the cemetery.

After the brief graveside service, people gathered in small groups, exchanged greetings and, in some cases, caught up on events in each other's lives. Dave and I lingered by the grave, not saying much. Finally, I looked up to find everyone had drifted back to the line of cars. They were waiting for us to get in the limo so we could all drive to the luncheon. I pointed this out to Dave and, hand in hand, we slowly started moving away from the flower-strewn coffin.

Suddenly, Dave turned to me and threw himself into my arms, a child sobbing for his mother. I hugged him tightly and cried for Jean, too, but selfishly, I also wept for myself.

I wept for the loss of my dear mentor and friend. I railed against the capricious genetic error that reduced that feisty woman to a docile one stroking the cat, depriving us of her warmth and wisdom. Everyone spoke in terms of her tragic accident. I wondered then if that were the case, and I wonder about it still. The questions haunt me: Was her death purely accidental? A set of coincidences twisted together in her failing mind? Or was it her deliberate choice?

I like to think she bravely chose the light.

Contributors' Notes

Jan L. Backes spent her childhood in the maze of post WWII streets known as Levittown, PA. She lives in Plymouth Meeting, PA with her partner, Flo, of thirteen years. Jan's hobbies include photography and an avid interest in covered bridges. Three things she cannot live without are: God, sobriety and a peaceful home life. Her poem, "Birdsoar," was published in a poetry anthology by The International Library of Poetry and she was featured on the home page of www.poetrysoup.com twice in 2011. She enjoys her experience in the Women's Writing Circle. "I'm not afraid to share my darkest moments. I know my words will be met with open arms."

Maureen Barry is a storyteller and the author of six children's books. Her stories can be found on her website www.maureenbarry.com. "I love to create original stories, then bring them to life in a performance. Children are magical as their imaginations run with my stories. My memoir is presently a work-in-progress and I plan to publish it. Everyone has a story to tell. Our stories connect us to each other and help us understand how life acts upon us. It is the connection between people that keeps me intrigued."

Maureen was a teacher for over thirty-three years at the high school and college levels, and was involved with theater productions in the classroom and on the stage. Maureen facilitates workshops in the art of storytelling, writing children's books and memoir. She sails, travels and lives in Malvern, PA.

Lynda M. Clemens is co-author of *Hit the Job Running: Because landing the job is the easy part*, 3rd edition, written to help recently laid off employees succeed in a new position. As a recent retiree from three decades doing Information Technology projects for large corporations, Lynda has chosen fictionalized memoir as her next challenge. "I want to share my life's lessons with others. Perhaps they can glean some valuable insights into their own lives." A Philadelphia native, she currently volunteers with an adult literacy program and is a member of the Women's Writing Circle in Chester County where she resides. Lynda holds a Ph.D. in Educational Psychology from Temple University. She has been an adjunct faculty member at Penn State Great Valley School of Professional Studies, Arcadia University, Temple University and Drexel University.

Kimberly Ely is the author of several short stories, including "When Professionals Carry Diaper Bags," "Pizza is a Real Toot," and "The Gardener's Daughter." She has been a freelance writer since 2007, publishing for Spirit Magazine and The Dog Street Journal. She works as a copy editor for a charter school and is pursuing an MFA in fiction at Arcadia University. She resides in Downingtown, PA with her husband, Mark.

Sharon Keys Gray is an information technology professional who writes in her leisure. Her writing includes poetry and fiction. She lives in Chester County, PA with her husband Bob, their youngest son Jeremy and the family's collie Siegfried.

Patty Kline-Capaldo earned a BA in Journalism and History from Indiana University and teacher certification from Ursinus College. A National Novel Writing Month winner in 2011, Patty enjoys writing short stories, memoir, and the occasional poem. But most of her writing energy is focused on finishing her first novel. Patty resides in Pottstown, PA with her husband, Rich, and their three cats, Sarah, Splash, and Snapple. She hosts Just Write (www.meetup.com/Just-Write-in-Collegeville-PA/, a weekly writers' group.

Vicki McKeefery graduated from Penn State with a bachelor's degree in Psychology and from Villanova University with a master's degree in American History. She lives in Malvern, PA and works for the Chester County Historical Society in West Chester, coordinating their youth and family programs. An educator for twenty-five years, she began her career teaching history in secondary school and finished by working as a reading specialist in elementary school. She likes to read, write, and walk the trails of Chester County in her free time.

Jodi Monster is a writer living in Berwyn, PA. She is the author of a memoir and several short stories and essays. Prior to settling in suburban Philadelphia, she and her family lived in The Netherlands, Texas and Singapore. She is a graduate of Dartmouth College and the University of Chicago. Many of Jodi's stories, including the one in this anthology, take place in an anonymous, seaside town in southern New England because the landscape there, with all its drama and beauty, is the most worthy backdrop she can imagine for the inherent drama and beauty of women's lives.

Ginger M. Murphy is a citizen advocacy coordinator, community organizer and true believer in the promise and power of civic engagement. She has worked as an English teacher, tutor and grant writer and holds a master's degree in education from the University of Pennsylvania. "I like to explore how our voices begin to emerge as we dare to tell our own unique stories. I write to discover the deeper layers of my experience; to sift, sort and discover a reflection that holds personal and universal experiences all at once." An avid hiker and photographer, she lives in Phoenixville, PA with her three wise feline housemates.

Edda R. Pitassi has maintained a love/hate relationship with writing since she started seeing her "letters to the editor" in print at age fifteen. A published journalist with several suburban newspapers, she currently contributes a monthly book review for *Chester County Seniors!* newspaper. A former web content writer and proofreader, her employment history includes a 20-year career with IBM. Highlights of her writing life comprise a writing internship in New York City, editing *Morning at Wellington Square*, and contributing to the Women's Writing Circle.

Flo Shore has spent eighteen years in industrial sales. She also spends time as a part-time professional pet sitter affording her the opportunity to express her love of all creatures. As a pet sitter Flo cares for cats, dogs, and some exotics such as fancy rats and occasional farm animals as well. She enjoys nature, hiking, camping, travel and adventure. Flo is also the mother of a lovely 27-year-old daughter. "I have been writing poetry since childhood and am relatively new to prose. My introduction to memoir through the Women's Writing Circle has proved invaluable."

Harriet Singer is an Energy Healer, Reiki Master and hospice volunteer. She is a member of the Women's Writing Circle and has been writing poetry for three years. This is her first published work.

Candice L. Swick is a graduate of West Chester University where she earned her BA in American Literature. She lives in Downingtown, PA and has enjoyed writing poetry since she was a teenager. In 1999, Candice had a poem published in The Poetry Guild's anthology, "A Shimmer on the Horizon." For the last year, she has been a member of the Women's Writing Circle. Candice is currently pursuing an interest in writing short stories and possibly a memoir.

Susan G. Weidener is the author of two books, *Again in a Heartbeat, a memoir of love, loss and dating again*, and the sequel to that, *Morning at Wellington Square*. "I like to write about our choices as women and our lives, our struggles and accomplishments. I also write about the search for love, this quest for passion, renewal and magic, which is the heart of any romantic."

A former reporter with *The Philadelphia Inquirer*, Susan has interviewed a host of interesting people from all walks of life, including Guy Lombardo, Bob Hope, Leonard Nimoy and Mary Pipher. An experienced book editor and teacher of writing workshops, Susan founded the Women's Writing Circle, a support and critique group for writers in suburban Philadelphia. She lives in Chester Springs, PA. Her website is: www.susanweidener.com

Diane Yannick grew up in the 1950's in Newark, DE. She uses many of her childhood experiences as material for her writing. She joined the Women's Writing Circle in 2010 and feels that it has helped her find her voice. She taught language arts for 33 years at both elementary and secondary public schools in Pennsylvania, Delaware and Maryland. After retiring for medical reasons, she began to tutor beginning readers in her home. She often goes back into classrooms as a storyteller. Diane likes to garden, quilt, knit, read, and play the piano. She started her own book club about four years ago. She lives in West Chester, PA with her husband, John.

Melinda Sherman, editor, grew up in northwestern Ohio. After graduating from Miami University with a BA in Victorian Literature, Melinda moved to New York City and lived in Manhattan for 17 years. She received a master's degree from Columbia University. She worked as a production assistant at Warner Books before moving to Walker & Company as a senior editor in the educational materials division. She subsequently worked for Macmillan & Company and Scholastic. After a 10-year hiatus to raise her children, Melinda became an ESL (English as a Second Language) instructor in an adult education program. She has taught journal writing and memoir writing workshops for more than 10 years. For seven years Melinda has been an adjunct professor of English at Suffolk County Community College on Long Island. She is also a student in the MFA in Writing & Literature Program at Stony Brook University in Southampton.

Jane Choc, illustrator, is a native of Chester County, PA. A graduate of the Studio School of Design in Philadelphia, she then attended the University of the Arts for two years, followed by two years of study in painting, drawing and sculpture at The Pennsylvania Academy of Fine Arts.

Jane creates custom paintings in watercolor and pen and ink of homes, businesses, churches and institutions. Jane specializes in portraits that have special significance to her clients. She designed the cover of this book based on photographs of the women who have attended the Women's Writing Circle and her pen and ink drawings in the book reflect the book's themes of childhood, career, motherhood, relationships and aging. Her website is: www.janechoc-ink.com/

About The Women's Writing Circle

The Women's Writing Circle is a support and critique group for writers living in the Philadelphia area. The group meets for readings the second Saturday of the month and for critique the last Saturday of the month.

The goal is to provide writers a place to share their work in a spirit of camaraderie and goodwill, as well as discuss the craft of writing and publishing options.

The Women's Writing Circle also offers workshops in creative writing, memoir, journaling and independent publishing. Workshops are open to men and women.

For more information, go to www.susanweidener.com or visit the Women's Writing Circle on Facebook at: https://www.facebook.com/WomensWritingCircle

Made in the USA
Charleston, SC
22 April 2013